The Picts of Scotland

Clayton N. Donoghue

FriesenPress

Suite 300 - 990 Fort St
Victoria, BC, V8V 3K2
Canada

www.friesenpress.com

Copyright © 2017 by Clayton N. Donoghue
First Edition — 2017

Edited by: Darrell M. Bright B.A. B.Th. and Holly Foley

ISBN
978-1-4602-9288-4 (Hardcover)
978-1-4602-9289-1 (Paperback)
978-1-4602-9290-7 (eBook)

1. HISTORY, EUROPE, GREAT BRITAIN

Distributed to the trade by The Ingram Book Company

Table of Contents

List of Illustrations

The Romans called them Pictae and the Irish called them Cruthni. In the modern world we have accepted an abbreviated Roman version as simply The Picts. Now that there has been over 40 books written, a dozen TV documentaries and two motion pictures on them it is getting kind of hard to say they are a mysterious people any more. However, from all the recent excitement on them still there is a lot to be learned about them. From what I have found in my personal research on the Picts is the origins is still being very much glossed over. Many historians are still claiming they are a pure culture onto themselves which isn't true at all.

The Picts emerged from the evolution of two cultures that came together in 450 BC. The first culture was an extremely old one and they are commonly identified as simply the "UrnField People". These were a prehistoric people who built Stonehenge some 4500 years ago. The second group is called the Halsatt Celts. They migrated into what we now know as Scotland around 450 BC. From the mixing of these two people scholars believe circa 200 BC evolved what we now identify as the Picts. As always the Picts did not call themselves Picts that was a name the Romans gave them circa 78 AD. By Celtic tradition they would have referred themselves by the name of the tribe they came from, such as Novantae or Calidonii. In much the same way as the North American Indians did for example the Iroquois referred themselves by their tribal names like Mohawk and Seneca.

Briefly what these two cultures represented when merged together was a type of people that admittedly is unique from the rest of Europe. The Picts were able to preserve elements of the Urnfield nation and bring it forward in time where today particularly in the language. The language once thought to have completely disappeared is now slowly making a comeback. In the research scholars are now realizing certain words are neither Celtic nor anything else except perhaps a prehistoric. From this aspect alone the Picts are growing in popularity with ancient researchers. Thus if the language has been able to preserve elements of a much older culture then maybe other parts of the culture were too. In this book I am going to show what those other identities were. Scotland today you can physically see where the Halstatts begin and end and where too the Urnfield People begin and end. The mountain range that basically cuts through the centre of the country from north to south is the divide line between the two nations. All along the east coast was the Halstatt Celts and all along the west was the "Urnfield People". Where the two people merged was in their political and cultural practices. Here it can only be identified as uniquely Pict.

Of course what most people are excited about the Picts is their legendary reputation as being ferocious warriors. It is undeniable the Romans could not suppress them in the usual manner of bribery and brutality; so they resorted to simply building a massive wall the width of modern day Scotland infamously known as Hadrian's Wall. As you will find out the great wall was not very successful in keeping the Picts out of Roman Britain. Over a period of 400 years the Picts crossed into Britain no less than a dozen times, not to mention the fact they also had an enormous navy of over 400 small ships that sailed around the wall and sacked the east coast on hundreds of occasions. Though the Romans and later the Saxons were able to repel for a majority of the incursions they were unable to contain them. The Picts were relentless, determined and as mentioned before ferocious in battle. Going through their history it is an amazing wonder how a people who it seemed was forever fighting was able to survive as a people. Yet they did. As a distinct culture they existed from roughly 200 BC to 800 AD. It appears that when they were finally conquered by the famous Kenneth MacAlpin is when at last they began to fade as a nation.

However, having said that recent research has shown the Picts may very well still be with us today through the modern day Scot. The world of science is revealing things never known before and it comes as no surprise from this source the Picts haven't quite disappeared. In this book I hope to show some of these new aspects and as well such should prove inspirational. So sit back and enjoy.

CHAPTER 1

Disaster at Mons Graupius

To plunder, to slaughter, to steal, these things they misname empire; and where they make a wilderness, they call it peace.

TACITUS

The year is 77 AD and a man by the name of Gnaeus Julius Agricola has just arrive in Roman Briton. He was the newly appointed Roman Governor just sent by Emperor Vespasian. Along with him was his young nephew Cornelius Tacitus who was to be employed as the governor's official historian. Tacitus's writing of Agricola's campaign managed to survive and as such we have a firsthand account of basically the very first encounter the western world has with the Picts. Mind you the embellishment throughout the story is at times even hard for the Romans to stomach let alone us today.

Roman Briton at this point in time was still not fully conquered. The Island was a patch work of unreliable client states like the Brigantes in central Briton, some direct control states like the Iceni in the south east of Briton, independent states in the west like the Ordovices and way up in the north a strange savage like people called the Calidonii, nicknamed as Pictae. They got that name specifically from Tacitus because their bodies were tattooed in blue ink. The emperor gave instructions to Agricola he wanted the mishmash of Briton to be cleaned up and simply have the entire Island completely under Roman control. To Agricola a very experienced Roman field general with a pragmatic personality thought the task as routine. He felt so confident in the mission he even had on his agenda of conquering the Irish in the process. He figured he could get the whole thing done in under five years. Agricola felt he could be back in Rome no later than 83 AD at the latest parading thousands of slaves and wagons full of gold just like Julius Caesar back in the days of the Gaul Campaigns of 55 BC.

Tacitus does not tell us where Agricola began his mission but it's more than likely it started in the massive Roman garrison of Camulod just north of Londinium (London) on the east coast. Here Agricola assembled an army and a navy for the task. He was not leaving anything to chance. His army comprised of two over strength professional legions, the 9th and the 20th with three under strength legions of infantry auxiliaries and two auxiliary cavalry "squadrons" (3,000 horse). According to Tacitus he estimate the entire entourage including supply wagons to about 30-35,000. When we find out how quickly he marches off it would seem Agricola was also a very efficient organizer. It was only a matter of months when he was off on the road.

Agricola decided he first destination was the Ordovices up in the North West corner of modern day Wales (Gwenyd). The Ordovices were still a holdout Celtic nation who thought their mountainous terrain could fight off the Romans in much the same way the Silures did down in the south east corner of Wales. The Silure managed to secure the status of becoming a Roman client state when they ended their fighting in 65 AD. If push came to shove the Ordovices were hoping for the same when Agricola showed up at their front door.

Agricola assembled his army at Deva (Chester) Wales and tried to see if there could be some form of way to negotiate with the Ordovices into the Roman Empire. As it turns out the Ordovices arrogantly said no to all the offers. Tacitus accounts is Agricola simply became frustrated and marched on them. Tacitus makes it sound like it was an easy slaughter for the Romans yet when you examine the time line of how long it took you wonder if this is not his first big embellishment of Agricola's success. It isn't till the following year when at last Agricola finally defeats the Ordovices. A full year of fighting does not sound like a cake in the park. Further, the outcome you wonder if that was the way it really went. When you look into the Ordovices some 400 years later when Maximum Maximus is Governor; the Ordovices are a full client state and are such an independent one that can easily afford to lend warriors to the governor in his campaign in Gaul, it makes you wonder what really happened. There is no evidence of a crushed people as Tacitus would have you believe.

Well whatever the circumstance the fact remains by the end of 83 AD the Ordovices were now part of the Roman Empire. Agricola when he gets back to Deva decides to split his army. The 9th Legion stays in Deva while the 20th is to march to a place called Eburacum well inside Brigante territory. The Brigantes were officially a client state, but over the years their loyalty could never be guaranteed. When the Agricola showed up on their front door they were said to have been in a rebellious mood. So once more another Celtic nation had to be subdued. And like before Tacitus described the campaign in magnificent psychedelic glorious detail. Agricola was the soldier of soldiers. I am willing to bet if he knew what was being written about him he would have likely told his young nephew to tone it down.

Anyways, once the Brigantes are brought firmly under Roman control Agricola now continues his march north. The next Celtic nations which were much independent were the Novantae and Selgovae in what is now Northumbria. Agricola methodically subdues them too and it takes him well over a year to get through their countries. Though Tacitus tells of awe inspiring feats of Roman military superiority the time period seems desperately slow for such easy victories.

In the winter of 79 AD Agricola sent word to his navy to come up the east and west coast for supplies and coastal support. He reassembles his two legions of the 9th and the 20th with his auxiliaries on the Caledonian boarder. Over the winter he starts to strategize how he is going to now deal with the most unknown group of natives on the Island. His intelligence tells him the Pictae are a ruthless savage like animals. In fact rumor has it they are cannibals. Apparently Tacitus tells us leaving nothing to chance he sends out a sweeping reconnaissance of the southernmost part of Calidonian country to get a feel of whole the Pictae are all about. The scouts come back reporting they have found nothing; so cautiously Agricola moves forwards into what is called "The trackless waste". The Roman advance falls mysteriously silent at this point in the operations. It takes Agricola a whole year to travel only 100 km and reaches the modern area of Glasgow and Edinburgh.

Agricola wants to clear the area around Glasgow and have a firm base for his ship and men for when he decides to invade Ireland. Tacitus tells us he had his first big run in with the locals here. There isn't much in the way of details again only that Agricola is compelled to use his entire combine force to subdue the beach area. However, things must have been far different then what was reported for we learn that by the year 82 AD Agricola's forces are dramatically smaller. You see when it comes to the Romans they kept ledgers of their everyday accounts. It didn't matter what Tacitus wanted to exaggerate on the fact is the actual Roman records were available and they definitely told a completely different story.

Here is one such example of when you compare Tacitus writing verse Roman records. Back in 77AD Tacitus described Agricola's army of being well over 30,000 men. When Agricola was now lining up his men to cross the Firth of Forth in 82 AD his military force was now a little then 20,000. Tacitus makes no mention of how some 10,000 Roman soldiers suddenly disappear from the ranks. Yet the Roman legers do. They do not tell what battles were fought only that on certain dates large groups of troops no longer existed. They clearly reflect Agricola was not having an easy time of it as he continued to move north.

In the spring of 83 AD Agricola decides he will once again split his forces the 9th Legion will march out on his left flank and he will march up the east coast of Calidonii territory with the 20th. Tacitus says that for the first time the Pictae came out in great force and attacked Agricola's column. He immediately went to ground and called for the 9th for help. Yet something must of happened to the messengers for it turns out the 9th legion did not come to Agricola's aid.

The 9th Legion it turns out continued marching all day with no interruption. Clearly by their action they had no idea what was going on with the 20th. They marched a good 20 km when they decided to stop and build a temporary "Marching Camp" at a place known as Darnoch. Romans it seemed could build a wooden palisade fortress in a matter of hours. I suppose with a force of over 5,000 men that wasn't very hard. As it was the 9th legion of having a relatively inactive day settled in for the night. Agricola was only 20 km to the south east at a place called Abernethy. Frustrated with the lack of response by the 9th Agricola decided that in the middle of the night he will march his legion to rejoin them.

Just before twilight horns could be heard all around the 9th Legion's camp. Then out of the dark came thousands of screaming Picts rushing over the walls. The Romans were complete taken by surprise. For the next hour of so the legion was being slaughtered. The Picts were having an easy time of the confused and half asleep Legionnaires. In the mayhem it looked like it was all over for the Romans as the Picts came down on them on all sides. Just as the final breath of what was left of the few Romans still standing, another set of horns were heard followed by a powerful rhythm of drums. It was Agricola. He came just in the nick of time. Upon seeing the arrival of the Roman rescue force the Picts fled at once. The Picts it would seem knew instinctively never to fight the Romans in their terms. Tacitus of course claims hundreds of Picts were killed as they tried to make their get-a-away. But had to admit it was scary to see how fast it was for them to disappear into the woods.

For mysterious reasons we don't know what became of the 9th Legion, only that what was ever left of them was amalgamated into the 20th. It would seem from this point on we are totally dependent on Tacitus's writings and nothing else. People often get this event mixed up with the infamous even of 108 AD where the 9th was again sent into Caledonii but this time they never returned. The reason people get this impression is because Tacitus never mentions this legion again. As such the two different events often get confused with each other.

Agricola found himself in a near disaster and had to regroup quickly. He desperately heads for the sea to get in contact with his fleet with what is left of his army. His intelligence tells him he is now badly outnumbered and being totally wiped out is a strong reality. He heads for a place known as Darnoch about 25 km away on the east coast. Along the way every 5-6 km he stops and quickly built a marching camp; so he was moving incredibly slow and not taking any chances. A total of 4 marching camps were built before he finally reached the shore line. If we can assume it takes about a day to build a marching camp then it is easy to know it took at minimum of 4 days to reach the beaches.

Tacitus tells us Agricola has more auxiliary re-enforcements once on the beach; so it can be assumed the troops came off the ships. We are told that Agricola's forces are back up to the strength of 20,000 men. This number implies, but of course with no certainty, around 4,000 were lost in the night attack.

No doubt Agricola was definitely angered by the surprise attack and the enormous hit he took from it, he wasn't wasting time in getting back on the road. However, it was an all-new approach. First he was not separating his forces again and second he was now staying close to the shore line where his fleet was always in sight. Third that little building blitz of marching forts proved to be an effective approach in safe guarding his men. Thus he decided to go that route as now he started his deep march into Pictae territory. Tacitus tells us Agricola now had a far more determine attitude than ever before to conquer Calidonii.

With his reinforcements Agricola found his army stretched for about 20 km; so he decided that will be where the next marching camp will be located. Thus when the last Roman was leaving the safe guards of one fort their front rank was building the next. It would seem the Picts had figured out Agricola's strategy. Tacitus writes that as they were just starting to build their next camp that is when the Caledoniis would strike. The Romans in time were realizing that once the front rank stopped to quickly call up for reinforcements. They knew the Picts would soon strike yet again. It was guerrilla warfare pure and simple. To the Romans it was frustrating in the dense forest fighting the Picts. Open field combat is what the Legionnaire more familiar with.

This form of monotonous fighting was draining on the Roman resources. Agricola found that under the circumstances he was compelled to send part of his ships back to Gaul and for resupply. Historians have learned the General was in particularly bringing in boat loads of nails. Apparently his new style of fighting was turning into an exhausting expensive operation of building. By 83 AD Agricola had built 7 marching camps and only progressed 100 km into Calidonia. The Picts kept to their same strategy the whole way through. Once the army was stretched to its limit and was just about to build its next fort the Pict would again strike. In Tacitus writings you could see even he was getting exasperated with the slug fest. You could not pin down the Picts and with it everything was grinding down to a crawl. By the winter of 83-84 the Romans made it to a place called Raedykes. Hugging to the shore line Agricola was about 140 km away from the Caledonian capital itself of Inverness. Yet Tacitus writings give us no clue that Agricola was aware he had come so close to the heart of the Pictae nation.

It is by the end of this year we at long last get the name of who is leading the Pictish forces and he is Calgacus. Tacitus says that on two separate occasions Calgacus and Agricola had it out but we don't know where only that Agricola was triumphant on both encounters. Does seem a little strange why Calgacus would do that when he was having far better success in his hit and run tactics. Some historian's feels Tacitus was getting desperate and simply invented these two fights to at long last give his uncle some tiny form of fame. Finally when the snow starts to fall Agricola decides he will pull back his main force some 100 km to Abernethy. There is no reasoning for this other than simple safety. He leaves about 500 men at each of the 7 garrisons built so far. Archaeologists today back up that claim so that would mean some 3500 troops were strung along the coast and the remaining 16,500 were withdrawn from the front so to speak.

The following spring Agricola was once again hard at it. He would march his troops 15-20 km and start building another marching fortress. He ends up building another ten camps at another distance of 120 km. So if we go by previous year's level of accomplishment it would put us approximately in the end of fall, start of winter. Tacitus tells us that Agricola in his last piece of the march he got an unexpected lucky break where he came upon a Caledonii granary. This seems a little hard to believe when the Picts did not have granaries. Anyways, staying with his interpretation the Picts knew they had to have it out with the Romans for now they were looking at a winter of starvation.

Agricola's Campaign March

At a famous place known as Mons Graupius –which no one to date has ever found – the Picts were massing an army. Word got back to Agricola and with no delay he galloped off. In his hurry he took with him on his auxiliaries and left behind the 20th legion. (*Seems unbelievable he would do that, but who cares, let's keep going*). When he arrived he found his troops lined up in a valley and up on a far ridge were said to be over 30,000 Pict warriors. And before I forget, Tacitus was there too. Also, to make things really exciting Tacitus tells us only15,000 troops were facing the enemy. So it had all the hallmarks this was going to be a desperate battle for survival. The Romans were not only badly outnumbered but were primarily comprised of loosely discipline auxiliaries. Everything looked like an easy victory for the Picts.

At this point it probably wise to let the reader know that this is all Tacitus. His artistic license goes into over drive and it really does become uncharacteristic of the usual sober Roman writing style. You have to remember Tacitus at this time was a really young man and felt it was necessary to really flash things up a bit to make to make a victory all the more glorious. We will find out later when the emperor reads his account even he has a hard time swallowing it.

Now that you know this we can now continue with Tacitus's story.

As the two armies stared each other down and the tension began to rise who should show up front on the top of the hill but non-other than Calgacus himself. He turns to his men and gives an awe inspiring speech that this is their last stand. Oddly enough Tacitus who cannot speak a word of Gaelic is close enough to the great warrior is able to catch every word (*again, as ridiculous as this really is, let's keep going*). Just as Calgacus finishes his heart moving speech the Picts start to descend down the hillside. Agricola, has his infantry in tight formation and sends his cavalry squadrons to the rear. Calgacus instructs his warriors to flank out and it looks like they are going to completely encircle the defenseless Romans. Then Agricola screams out the order and outcome the cavalry! 15,000 horsemen gallop around the left flank and another 15,000 horsemen crash around the right flank. The Picts take one look at the racing cavalry and in an instant they flee back up the hill. The cavalry

chase them down and miraculously manage to slay over 10,000 Picts. In this remarkable piece of incredible luck the Romans only manage to suffer 350 dead. When the smoke clears there are only the Romans standing. Some 20,000 Picts simply disappear into the woods. For Agricola this is very disappointing. He knows at once he has no slaves to take back to Rome; nor does he have Calgacus to ceremonially strangle in the coliseum. So what does he do? On his march back to Abernethy he manages to stumbles into a hapless tribe of about a 100 Otadinii Britons and quickly snatches them up as his campaign prisoners. Of course this gets quickly uncovered when they get back to Rome.

That winter Agricola is back to his winter quarters in Abernethy tries to figure what he will do next. He somehow knows his time has run out. Sure enough that very spring to his utter regret, Centurion arrives to tell him he is being summoned back to Rome. If you were in Agricola's position you know this is bad. By Roman standards Agricola had absolutely nothing to show for his campaign. Again if you take a moment to look at Julius Caesar's Gaul campaign you will readily see the difference. When Caesar came back to Rome he had over 20,000 Gaulic slaves, he had dozen of wagons filled with gold and last but not least he had the leader of the Gaul's Versingetorex himself. He was the hero of all heroes and the Romans just loved him! To say Agricola was in serious trouble is an understatement.

From the instruction given to Agricola, Rome was not fully aware at the true state his Briton forces were in. Rome had incurred some problems along the German boarders and they wanted him back with his two legions to deal with it. It was taken for granted Agricola had still fully intact two full legions and they were now needed elsewhere. The idea that the 9th had almost been wiped out would easily come as a horrible shock. Right there and then Agricola knew he was going to have to do a lot of explaining. Luckily from here we now can rely on Roman records to see how Emperor Vespasian responded to the seven long years Agricola was away. At long last we get some sense of what really took place.

By mid-summer of 85 AD Agricola, Tacitus and the 20th Legion with a hundred sad looking Briton slaves arrived in the great capital of the mighty empire. We find out there is no celebration upon their arrival; so that should say a lot right there. It would appear with no surprise the Emperor was tipped off on the true state of affair and Agricola's entourage once home are quickly brought in through the back door. Vespasian was served with Tacitus's historical account of the entire operation and it was a lengthy document. Upon reading it the Emperor's immediate reaction was said to be laughter. Agricola's response was he exploded in anger. Under normal circumstances the emperor would have had the Governor arrested for disrespect but the two men it turns out were good friends so the emperor simply told him to calm down. Then he turned to the young Tacitus and boldly told him the account he wrote was nothing short of ridiculous. In fact the emperor told poor Tacitus the battle of Mons Graupius was nothing short of sheer fabrication. It does explain a lot when you consider to this day they have never found the battle site.

Tacitus was for the first time at a loss for words as the Emperor explained to him that if the battle of Mons Graupius really did happen it would have followed a typical well recognized manner of fighting every Roman knew. First he explains, auxiliaries are never employed in the tight Roman box formation because they have never been trained to do that only regular professional troops would know how to do that. Also, auxiliaries are primarily made up of barbarians like the Picts and as such don't have the discipline to pull it off. Auxiliaries as the Emperor points out are employed in the front rank in a single line to fire a single volley of spears and then draw the enemy back to the main body where the professionals finish them off. Tacitus who had no military background was clearly unaware of the fundaments to the Roman military infrastructure and as such did not know how the various elements of line infantry and auxiliaries would have been realistically employed. Here alone his reporting crashes badly.

The Emperor then turns to Agricola and says that the young Tacitus has claimed that after the battle Agricola went on to completely conquer the whole country. Of course by Roman accounting practices this could be easily proven if it were true. By Roman policy it was to take 1/3rd of all booty and slaves from the population at large. Since the Pict population was not known then you have to work with what was and in this case it was their military. Seeing the Picts had an army of 30,000 men there must be a t least 10,000 slaves. Agricola had only a hundred slaves and they weren't even Picts. Then of course the most favourite subject of the Romans is the fame Pictish gold. Reliable sources claimed the Picts did have gold and modern archaeologist found that the Roman belief that the Picts did have it is well founded. Scotland today still has a gold vein down in the region of Argyle. As we know Agricola did not have so much of a grain of gold to show for his conquest. So that is two strikes against the general. Last but not least the terms of surrender were the leader of the enemy (Calgacus) to physically surrender himself personally to the Romans. To the Romans the fallen leader of an enemy being paraded down the main street of Rome had a huge symbolic meaning. Calgacus as we know was never taken prisoner. As such on the symbolic side of things it is with good reason the Picts were never defeated. Then the last and biggest concern of all that would surely bring the scorn of the senate and that was what happened to the 9th Legion? Roman records do not mention this subject at all and again it is for good reason why. The loss of a Legion is deemed as the ultimate disgrace. It is so disgraceful it's not even recorded. We find when after being rebuilt the 9th is again wiped in Briton in 108 AD the exact same scenario happens again; the Romans simply don't record it. If it were not for the fact Agricola and Vespasian were good friends the truth is Agricola's military career would have ended right there and then.

Only because Vespasian was in a tense situation with a barbarian uprising with Germanic tribes, he needed all the competent commanders he could get his hands on and Agricola despite his dismal failure with the Picts he was still highly regarded. Since the Governor was still valuable to Rome Vespasian needed a public event to make the Governor look good once more in front of the public. As it was a major parade was elaborately orchestrated and Agricola was public proclaimed the great conqueror of the Pictish "Emperor Calgacus" and to mark his great victory, in the Roman province of Morocco a triumphal archway was built in his honour. A few years later a number of unlikely Picts were captured by Romans and dragged down to the dusty province and killed by wild animals in a make shift coliseum. So officially Agricola was herald as the great conqueror of the Picts. No doubt this was probably the best example anywhere in history where the spin doctors were at their very best. And what becomes tragically sad about the whole event is many historians' centuries later buy into the spoof reporting Agricola was indeed a great general when he was anything but.

Back in Caledonia; what Roman ranks were left were all pulled backed to the marching camp of Inchtuthil near the Abernethy. For about 5 years the Romans claimed they tried to rule the Picts with an auxiliary force of not more than 5,000 men. There are no records in any form that taxation ever took place. The simple truth is the garrison sat as a lonely outpost as nothing more than hollow symbol of Roman Imperial power. In the fifth year the remaining Roman presence was pulled back to where to be was built Hadrians Wall. The Romans again sent in the 9th Legion in 108 AD to punish the Picts and as everyone know they mysteriously disappeared never to be heard of again.

As mentioned leaving Vespasian out of the picture has what made Tacitus' written account of Agricola's campaign far more glorious than what it really was. Again when you do, it is puzzling archaeologists cannot find even a remote trace of where Mons Graupius existed. Not even the name is traceable. As such one is left to wonder did Tacitus make the whole thing up? Was Vespasium right when he said it was indeed a brilliant work of pure fabrication?

CHAPTER 2

The Urnfield People join with
the Hallstatt Celts

An honest man here lies at rest,
As e'er God with His image blest:
The friend of man, the friend of truth;
The friend of age, and guide of youth:
Few hearts like his, with virtue warm'd,
Few heads with knowledge so inform'd:
If there's another world, he lives in bliss;
If there is none, he made the best of this.

ROBERT BURNS

In order to understand who the Picts were you have to go back to the Neolithic age c. 3000 BC. Many authors prefer not to address the real origins of the Picts on account it can get as complicated as the Picts themselves. As it is they find the folklore origins a much easier route to go for there isn't very much to it. The intensity of the Scottish legend of the Picts, they were a cultural entity onto themselves known as "Cruthni". They came to ancient Scotland about c. 200 BC from a Scandinavian country indirectly identified as Norway. From this line of thinking it is the claimed the Picts are an indigenous people of the land. Unfortunately, this is completely false and misleading as being nothing more than someone's imagination gone wild.

The true story about the Picts is far more complicated involving an enormous amount of archaeological study to verify the facts. The Picts in the simplest terms are a people who emerged from the joining of two prehistoric cultures. In this case the first group is known as the "Beaker People" or as some would call them "Urnfield *People*". For the purpose of this book I am going to use the term Urnfield People. They came to Britain c. 3000 BC. The second people are the Halstatt Celts. They came to Scotland c. 500 BC. From this time on the two cultures evolved together to becoming what we identify now as the Picts. As stated in the very beginning it was the Romans who gave them this name about 78 AD. Not until around 500 AD did the Picts ever call themselves by this name. How the Pictish culture evolves is much in the same manner as the English people came about. They were the results of the Angles and the Saxons fully coming together circa 600 AD.

By understanding who the Urnfield People and the Halstatt Celts are can we see which culture made their contributions to the Pictish identity. One of the biggest identities to the Picts is their appearance; they are described as having their bodies covered in blue tattoos. Where did that come from and more importantly is it true? The second big identity that made them legendary was of course their fierce fighting capability. As we know it was so ferocious the Romans were out done by them and in the end was forced to build Hadrian's Wall to contain them. Once more, where did that identity come from? These two well-known traits of the Picts, just for openers, have their origins from the Halstatt Celts. However their architecture and unique form of art design many experts feels have its primary contribution from the Urnfield People. The Pictish language is by far the most fascinating to today's scholars and here it has been determined as one aspect that the contribution was equal from both primary cultures.

To get things started the Urnfield People were not the first in Scotland. 3000 BC the land was already inhabited by people scholars simply addressed as Neolithic. These people were actually far more sophisticated then they are given credit for. They were farmers for the most part, lived in square houses were the ones who built the Passageway stone graves sites. They had a much healthier life style then the Urnfield People did for the average life span was 50 years. Once the Urnfield People arrive, though technologically more sophisticated, the average life expectancy degenerated to 40 years.

Migration Route of Urnfield People

J.P. Mallory and the famous Michael P. Pearson are probably the two best sources to go to in knowing who the Urnfield People were. In the region of Holland and Denmark are today circa 3000 BC is where formally they recognise as when the great Urnfield People migration started. The migration headed west in two directions. The first one was up into Britain but was not very significant. A discovery of an Urnfield plank boat in Dover in 1992 gives us a clue why. This ocean craft was small and very unreliable in the water. Only under mild conditions could it have made it across the English Channel. It probably took an enormous amount of work to build it when flint axes were the primary tool for building in those days and as such not a whole lot were built. Thus the major reasoning the Urnfield Migration into Britain at this time was limited in size. The second and more sizable migration went into France where it stopped for a while in the south west portion of the country; then it moved onto to the Tarsus Valley of Spain and Portugal. Here the Urnfield People seriously evolved into a very technically advanced culture. They stayed in this region till 2500 BC when once again they migrated up into Ireland, England and finally Scotland. Based on the size of this mass migration their boating skills had dramatically improved. However, Archaeologists have yet to find a boat of this era to verify it.

The Urnfield People got the name from the fact of their unique design in an assorted variety of clay pottery. From what they ultimately accomplished the name doesn't seem hardly suitable. Their biggest claim to fame is undoubtedly Stonehenge. Stonehenge was built c. 2400 BC. The Urnfield People were by this time now fully established and their engineering skills were nothing short of spectacular. Some other major contribution they brought to Britain was in metallurgy, society structure, fort and road building. For the native Neolithic residence this was a fantastic cultural improvement they immediately embraced.

What has to be noted as we get into the Urnfield People is they simply didn't absorb the Neolithic culture into extinction. This did not happen at all. Like the Picts the Urnfield People evolved as partially being Neolithic as well. Two cultures merging together. For openers the Neolithic Britain's were very well established at farming and that skill was filtered into the Urnfield. Archaeologists have found that all the structures that surrounded the building of Stonehenge were definitely Neolithic and not Urnfield. The buildings were all square for openers. The food stuff was found to be grain, barley, pork and beef. There was almost no evidence of wildlife which was more an identity of the Urnfield. So it could be seen the Urnfield were stone builders but not the farmers. Also the fundamental tools like the deer antlers that dug the ground for Stonehenge and the other stone circles were clearly Neolithic. Finally the most interesting reasoning for the building Stonehenge was learned to be solely a Neolithic concept and not an Urnfield one. Unlike the Urnfield People the Neolithic People placed a great emphasises on burial customs. Their passage graves are a testimonial to that specific identity. As it is the Urnfield People adopted their burial rituals and added great monuments to the tradition. So knowing just these few opening points we quickly learn it was a give and take set up of the two cultures. It certainly wasn't a case of one absorbing another.

Now that we have mentioned Stonehenge here; we have arrived yet another argument that even the concept of stone monument this was too Neolithic concept and not an Urnfield People contribution. As stated the stone passage-way graves are where some Scholars feel the Neolithic had already refined the art of megalithic monumental building. However, where the argument falls short is the fact there is nothing to be found above ground until well after the Urnfield People arrived. Stonehenge seems to reflect that the Urnfield People had a better grasp of mass organization and a political infrastructure. In the intricate design workmanship could only have occurred as a result of group engineering credentials, something there was no evidence of in the Neolithic people. Here perhaps is where the Urnfield People made their strongest contributions. Besides Stonehenge other stone circles start to appear all over the British Isles. Scotland is said to have had a particularly high concentration of them. The carving of stones was a blend of skills that scholars feels was a joint collaboration of both cultures. The Neolithic people had the genius to shape a stone but the incredible feat of moving it is fully credited to the Urnfield People.

Thus we come to the amazing over all engineering skills that was distinctly Urnfield People. It was in Scotland where Andrew Young makes an incredible discovery as a testimony to the Urnfield People; technological contribution to the whole megalith building world. Down in the south east corner near the Northumbrian boarder is where a concentration of stone columns are found. Nearby the circles is found an enormous collection of stone balls all dating to 2000 BC. Each of the stone balls measures exactly 75 mm in diameter. Researching the site he came to the conclusion the stone balls were -stone- ball bearings. Andrew built a wooden track device and placed in them a similar series of his own stone balls evenly spaced. Then he placed a wood rails over them and a wooden bed where he laid on top of it sand bags of 3.3 tons in weight. With only 8 people he found you could move the weight with relative ease. From this experiment he believes this is how the Urnfield People were able to move the stones around in the building of Stonehenge. They are to this day still digging around Stonehenge and if they come across the same stone balls that were found in Scotland it will be a major breakthrough to how the structure was likely built. From this discovery all the conventional thought of rolling logs and sand bridges are now being rethought.

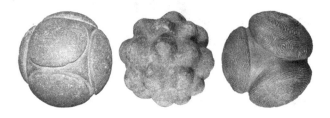

Examples of Urnfield Stone Balls

From this incredible accomplishment we learn they expanded on this in other areas and in doing so seriously changed the landscape. Thus many scholars feel they were the dominant culture which is true solely in the area of engineering. Staying with the passage grave for a moment we get to see some of the changes that take place on top of the visual arrangements. The Neolithic People used the passage stone graves to bury dozen of people in them. The Urnfield People preferred building mounds where only one or two persons were buried in them. Newgrange in Ireland is an excellent example of this. As it was two types of burial began to take place, distinction between the two cultures on the fundamentals. Further, cremations started coming into practice. Cremations were in its origins a Mediterranean custom. Next were the Ring Forts another Urnfield People invention. The need for defence was strictly an Urnfield People concept. The Neolithic Britain lived basically in a wooden village like structure communities for much of eastern and southern Scotland.

What "The Broch's" found on the west coast was to become an interesting contradiction of what was said of the Neolithic mentality when it came to forts. A broch was a large circular stone structure with a wall about 2 meters high and 20 meter in diameter with a stone circular tower in the middle about 5 meters high. At first glance it looks like a stone fort and appears the Neolithic shared similar values as the Urnfield People, but archaeologists examining them they were anything but militaristic. They found the structure could hold about 30 or so families and they lived inside the 2 meter wall. The centre structure was a kind of community centre where the little village of people gathered to cook and socialize. This was reinforced with the fact there was only small evidence of flint spear heads found.

Another big improvement to the Neolithic Britain is the coming of the Bronze Age to the Island. As it comes as no surprise the Urnfield People embraced it at once and so the Neolithic were forced to adopt it as well. J.P. Cummins in his book, *The Origins of the Irish,* has tons of evidence to show everything of the Neolithic Age People, was built in stone. Flint axes were the most prized tool for these people. The speed from which the Neolithic Briton adopted to the Bronze Age was equally fast. Again, what separates the Neolithic and the Urnfield was the interest in the metallurgy around bronze. The Urnfield went full speed ahead in working the material not only into weapons but also into very ornate jeweler. With bronze soon emerge gold. Here too all the credit is given to the Urnfield in developing it and having it as source to their economy. It was when the bronze came to its zenith, when scholars genuinely agree the Neolithic Age Culture of Briton disappeared altogether. Thus now at around 1000 BC it is completely an Urnfield People principle society.

With The Urnfield People now firmly in control they continued to expand to all parts of Britain, notably Scotland. Here it seems the Urnfield major contribution to the north was their Ring Forts. The Ring Forts it is felt may have been inherited by the Celts when they arrive however so far there is not much evidence to support this conclusion as of yet. The Urnfield Ring Fort was distinct. It had primarily one huge super-size round thatched roofed building in the centre and circled with a mound and ditch. By 800 BC it changes mildly where two or three buildings are in the perfectly round dirt mound wall. There were no wooden palisades along the top of the exterior mound as became an addition once the Celts arrived.

Urnfield Thatched Home

The peak of the Urnfield Age, so to speak ends in 900 BC. A natural phenomenon occurs and the temperature of Britain comes down dramatically for several decades and basically crop farming comes to an end. Everybody now is completely dependent on their livestock to survive. It is believed that the weather change was because of a volcanic eruption in Iceland. Something politically must happen when this environmental disaster occurred. The building of stone circles and mound burial sites all come to an abrupt end. The Age of the megaliths is now over. Most of the Urnfield population was in the fame Salisbury Plains. Starting in 800 BC a migration heads east and settles in the now province of Berkshire. Here we see there is now a whole new way of community living. Several small round thatched roof homes are built but with a significant angle on the back part in place of one single large one. Also, people are now burying their dead just outside their homes. The great burial centres are being abandoned all together. Things are simpler. The major signature of the burials now is what they contain. There are only four items in a burial site. The first one is an urn filled with cremated remains. Next is an urn with food in it. A third urn contains scent in it and finally a bronze dagger. That is all there is to the simple burial site and from it there is likely far less formality to a burial ceremony as compared to what archaeologists say was the case at Stonehenge.

Finally, what did the Urnfield People look like? For this is very important to know when the Celts arrive on the ground. A well preserved peat bog burial of a man and a woman was excavated in Denmark dated c. 2000 BC. The man was found clean shaven wearing a leather hat, a woollen tunic and a kilt like skirt. This was complemented with a cloak that became a trade mark to all Celts later on. But there was no brooch to the cloak that we often associated with the shoulder cloak. The woman had long hair that looked like it was well kept, meaning it was combed. She wore a short woollen tunic and a long woollen gown dress. She also had a sash cord down her side. Archaeologists found in Britain a half moon shape bronze razor blade that accounts for why the men were cleanly shaven.

Historians and archaeologists are in full agreement that starting in 600 BC a new cultural development was taking shape in Britain at large. The most notable aspect of this change was the invention of Iron. Yes, the Iron Age had started and it was coming into Britain but at a much slower pace than the Bronze Age did. Historians feel the Urnfield People of Britain were for reasons unknown resisting change. Specifically designed tools were appearing but clearly not locally made. The design was based in the Etruscan culture but definitely imported from the Austrian region of Europe. The style is said to be the earliest form of the Halstatt Celts. This was a new culture that was growing at alarming fast pace and only a hundred years away from starting its own mass migration across Western Europe.

Historians like Simon James in his book, *The Celts,* testifies the Celts were another people who were going through a cultural evolution seeing in they too were not a pure culture. Halstatt Celts were at this time still defined a mix of three, possible four, nations. They were Germans, Ionians, Scythians and a touch of Etruscans. The German and Scythian side of the Celt made them an extremely war like people. The Ionian and Etruscan side of the Celts were innovative especially in the art of metallurgy. From 600 – 500 BC they traded and spatially migrated out in Western Europe. Their effect could be seen far away as Scotland. The Celtic Tear Drop design sword was a much sought item all over central Europe. Not only was it stronger then the bronze sword being made of Iron, but by the way it was made. The metal was a folding process that proved to be even better than any weapon made by Mediterranean countries like Greece and Egypt.

Then at last it started. In 450 BC the first great Celtic mass migration/invasion rolled across Western Europe. To a certain extent it was similar to the Urnfield People in 3000 BC but with far more aggression to it. The Halstatt Celts flooded into Denmark, France, Spain, Ireland, England and finally into Scotland basically in one continuous push. The violent manner in which they moved lead many to conclude it was more of a conquest then it was a migration. However, when you see what the Romans wrote about the style of their migration in the time of Julius Caesar (55 BC) you can't help but observe it had to be a combination. The Celts with all of their possessions and families would simply get up and start to cross the land. Anyone who opposed their move would be quickly attacked and destroyed. Once the opposition was out of the way they quickly settled.

In Scotland the Halstatt Celts have been traced going up the east coast as far north as the Orkney Islands. Somewhere in 350 BC the Celts then began migrating to the west coast. Here is the point to note. For most of Europe and Britain the Urnfield people were assimilated into the Celtic culture. However, in Scotland a totally different phenomenon took place. For reasons still not explained the Halstatt Celts mixed with the Urnfield People. Technically you had a mixture of three distinct cultures merging into one Neolithic, Urnfield and Celt. Maybe Scotland was so remote and distance the Halstatt Celts were stretched to their limit and as such couldn't physically make the same impact as they did everywhere else. As such now they have to compromise and compromise they did. The Urnfields particularly in their architecture and Neolithic farming techniques came to be recognisable in the new Pict society that was now starting to evolve. The language became a mix as well, no longer was it the distinct Goidelic dialect as their counter parts in the south. Over the next 300 years it would evolve into a language all its own where even Bede and Columba both said it was not recognisable with any other language. Then of course there was now a new appearance to these new people. Tattoos in particular became their chief trade mark. A trait picked up from the Celts but with extreme exaggeration. The once somewhat peaceful Urnfield People had now changed to being more in comparison to their aggressive Celtic version but like the tattoos the aggressive warlike personality was far scarier. By the time Agricola and Tacitus arrived on the scene some 300 years later they both admitted Picts were a culture onto themselves.

Before we get too carried away with the Picts we have to take a short step back into knowing who the Halstatt Celts were. The Halstatt Celts, as mentioned evolved into a distinct culture circa 600 BC. They were of course from their origins being of Scythian and Germanic they had powerful rough bases to their existence. Meaning they were a warrior base nation. Violence was very much part of their makeup. Having said that, in addition it was found they had an incredible artistic side to them, where they made some spectacular art work and had the best known metallurgic skills anywhere in the known world at that time. The fame Hochdorf burial site in south east corner of Germany has given modern archaeologists their best references to knowing some of the customs of these early Celts. The Halstatt Celt had a royal system of leadership and when their kings died they were buried with great ceremony and pomp. However, for the common Celt it was found to be far less ceremonious. Bodies of this time frame were simply buried with the very minimal of artifacts like clay jars and the odd sword if the person was a warrior. Also there was no special spot of burial as was the custom of the Urnfield People. Celts it seem buried at random, their everyday people and once buried that was the end of it. The burial site would more often than not simply disappear from all memory until centuries later when a lucky archaeologist would happen to stumble across it. Halstatt Celts pagan religion is said to have had a huge assortment of gods and goddesses, nothing became really common with a certain deity until much later when the La Tene Celts emerged in 250 BC. In basic appearance a Halstatt Celt did have tattoos covering much of his muscular body. He wore a woollen pair of pants and often bare from the waist up. More often than not a warrior and skilled at riding a horse, a trait they picked up from their Scythian background. Lastly they were clean shaven except for a trait mark that carried on when they became La Tene and that is their fame Manchu moustache. The language they spoke was called Goedelic Gaelic. It's a very harsh guttural like language and modern Irish and Scot still has the same qualities of its ancient origins. Though they had developed a fine form of metallurgic and jewellery skills it was not seen much at the common level such as brooches. This was only reserved for the very well to do at this point in time. As such a Halstatt Celt was in simplistic terms seen as rough, callous and simple in both manner and in appearances.

So what changes occurred when the Celts migrated into the cold north of the Urnfield People? In terms of forts the building of them was much the same as the Urnfield except for two major changes. Forts were no longer perfectly circular any more. They were now oval and enormous in which dozens of thatched roof circular houses could be accommodated. The mounds were built twice as high as the Urnfield People's with wooden palisades. These forts were designed to defend against attacks. Definitely no longer just a simple village confine. The political infrastructure was a now a petty kingdom like set up with a local chieftain. Oddly enough it was democratic. The chieftain was elected to office based on their credential to properly lead. A chief could stay in power as long as he continued to make sound decision and didn't get scared or wounded in battle. All chiefs had to be physically perfect. And to add to this woman were politically equal to men. They even had the right to be warriors if they so choose.

All of these things were readily put in place when the Celts arrived in the east coast of the country where they the Celtic culture is most pronounced. On the west coast not so distinguishable were these features for once more there was a physical problem of no trees and the cold temperatures that prevailed from the ocean winds. Here it is said the Celtic culture got some renovations or perhaps some enhancement would be a better way to describe it. Nudity was not so readily seen as such both men and women when not in battle covered up. The famous trusses (pants) were the common wear of the men and long single piece woollen dress was the dress for women. The Celts adopted the shoulder cape from the Urnfield People, pinned together with a rudely designed long pin with a plate at the end. The plate in time started taking on some artistic design qualities but never match the Celtic brooches that become popular in about 100 AD.

Again the country was divided by a mountain range that went through the centre of the country. On the west coast of Scotland was that the Neolithic Broch design forts stayed the course. In fact the circular stone design fort lead to it being improved upon when an Irish King Eochaid Mugmedon comes along and improves the design by making it a 4 stories high tower. As it the Neolithic Age People come to survive in the structured garrison lay out. The Celtic influence on this side of the country was limited due to the natural barrier. It is what was saved the Urnfield People's culture as result. Since the likely cold winds coming off the Irish Sea discourage the Hallstatt Celts from coming over, there is no doubt here is where the two people came to an understanding in sharing their cultural differences. As such what we have now come to fully recognize what a Pict is, turned out to be was largely the result of geographic and environmental restriction.

As for the subject of the Pict religion it ended up following the principles of Druidism. Druidism is claimed to have developed in Anglesey Wales some 4000 years ago and had spread into the Urnfield north from which the Halstatt Celts adopted when they arrived. There is no evidence of any other type of religious practices discovered thus far to have been unique to either the Celts or the Urnfield.

Chapter 3

The Pict Kingdom

We are the Little Folk -- we!
Too little to love or to hate.
Leave us alone and you'll see
How we can drag down the Great!
We are the worm in the wood!
We are the rot in the root!
We are the germ in the blood!
We are the thorn in the foot!

Rudyard Kipling

According to Irish Legend when Niall of the Nine Hostages landed his army in Alba (Scotland) c. 380 AD he was met by three Pictish Kings. They were the King of Calidonii, the King of Vacomagii and the King of Maetae. Turns out that legend has a lot of credibility to it for at this time in history there was three major kingdoms of the

Picts; and the names were indeed Calidonii (Calidonia), Vacomagii (Vacomagi) and Maetae. As we know the Romans were the first to confirm Calidonia when Agricola marched into the Pictish lands in 80 AD. It is interesting that for a people who were simply dismissed as being nothing more than barbaric savages they were sophisticated enough to be organized into three major kingdoms.

In W.A. Cummins book, *The Age of the Picts*, he states that circa 350 BC the Picts went through a major political reorganization. By this time the Hallstatt Celt had been fully merged with the Urnfield People and much of the Celtic institution was adopted by the country at large. Up until this point in time the Pictish lands were divided into seven small provincial kingdoms. They were: the Fidach in the far North West (Sutherland), the Ce in the far north east (Clashmore region), the Fiotla in the north east (Aberdeen), the Fib and Kinrose in the central west (Argyl), the Fortriu in the south west (Renfrew) and the Circhenn in the south east (Fife). After 350 AD three over all kingdoms emerged, as mentioned, in the far north was Vacomagi, in the middle was Calidonii and on the Northumbrian boarder was the Maetae. The Romans rolled through the Maetae Kingdom so fast they did not even bother to pick up their name.

From this reorganization an overall elected High king (so to speak) came into existence and resided in Inverness. The system was completely Celtic. However, it must be remembered the style we are talking about is Hallstatt. This meaning these Celts were still very much into a royal dynasty arrangement. People who are familiar with the La Tene Celts would be aware their system was a warrior based kingdom. The most capable warrior was elected to be High King. There was no royal lineage with them. The

Hallstat Celts did have a royal lineage, but with the Picts it takes a very interesting twist to it.

The selection of the Pictish King is from a matriarchal royal line. And this is not in the conventional understanding of what the word means. There were no Queens in the Pictish royal court. What there was, was a High Princess. This system gets pretty bizarre by today's standards so you have to follow this closely to know how it works. In the Pictish royal court there are several young women who are officially recognised as having High Princess status. When they come of breeding age they are mated with several partners in a very short period of time. The objective is for the woman to become pregnant and the father to be unknown. This way it is fully claimed the child is from a matriarchal line. Once pregnant the woman is married to a prince, thus keeping the royal heritage intact. These two people have no claims to the throne what so ever. If the child born is a boy then that child has legitimacy to becoming a king. As can be expected there are several boys wondering around the court who were born in this type of arrangement and all are eligible to become the next ruler.

When the current king dies or is considered by the college of Druids no longer fit to rule and that happened quite frequently, they select from the group of boys who is most suitable to be the next king. The criteria is very sensible. The boy must be in his early manhood (age average 20-25) and have successfully done all the training required of a king to this point in time. So all the boys who are under age are not selected and also true any boys who are over 25. As it is the one thing the Picts have over all other kingdoms is underage monarchs and decrepit leaders which is often the case with normal royal lines. The boy with the best credentials is elected to be the next king. This becomes a major point to know on the real reason why the Romans had such a difficult time conquering the Picts versus the other Celtic nations in Britain. The young king is of course married to a preselected princess and the kingdom carries on. As can be seen with this system there is no dynasty to speak of in the conventional meaning like in Russia and China. Here in the Pictish world the royal couple's children may have a lineage if one of their boys meets the requirements when he comes of age. Chances are it's not likely because the boy's father will be known and this takes away from their Matriarchal set up. For a boy from an existing king to be made the next king is the exception, not the norm.

The only interesting part from this system is the boy's name. It comes from the newly married husband of his mother. So if the child's name is David and his mother's husband's name is Brian, the child will be named David MacBrian. As we know Brian is not the natural father of David.

Going through the Pictish Chronicles it is found the average length in office of any Pictish king was only seven years. A King Drust in the 6th century was one of the few exceptions of being allowed to rule for over 24 years. This would mean all the kings for the most part were young competent and physically fit to run office. There was no examples of any old or feeble kings allowed to rule.

When we look at when Agricola arrived in Briton another Celtic tradition was upheld to bring national unity in times of crisis and that was the election of war general. The Picts knew the High King in the Inverness capital was not always the most suited for leading men in battle; mind you he had enough training in the profession. As it was like when the Roman's came, everyone knew they had to have unity in the ranks to fight them; so in some cases as it was with the fame Calgacus he was elected to be the military commander only. Once the national threat was gone the war commander was automatically retired. We see that even the Le Tene Celts with Vercingetorix in Gaul this tradition carried on. His career unfortunately ended tragically.

In closing on this election of public office is that the system was a royal one, women selected to breed for the next king had to be certifiable of a royal line. The average girl in the street played no part in ever becoming a princess.

From understanding the royal system archaeologists have only recently come to understand the fame Pictish tattoos and marking in what really mean. Up until now much of it was believed to be religious symbols. It appears the unique stone carving designs seen all across the country represented a ranking system. It was Tacitus who unwittingly discovered it when he wrote the markings on the Pictish warriors were laid out in the same order as was seen on their stones. Thus this gave us the first clue of what they truly meant. Examination of Roman documents and the study of the stone columns a pattern was confirmed. There are on most stone columns like the Picard Stone in Aberdeenshire a zig-zag design at the top and below followed by animal carvings. The zig-zag design came in only three patterns, one was a "V" design on top a crescent moon shape, the next was a "Z" design where it was flanked by two circles and the third was again a "Z" design with a snake woven through the centre bar. These three symbols have been found to be found to dominate in certain regions of the country where scholars are now speculating they may represent the three kingdoms. The "V" logo is found primarily in the north; so could be the logo for the Vocomagi. The "Z" with circles is found in central Scotland so it could be the logo for the Calidonii and finally the "Z" with the snake which is the fewest found in the south of Scotland may be the logo for the Maetae People.

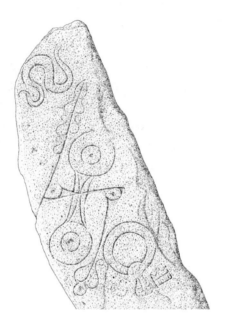

Pictish Carving Column

(Again, before you start to take away the thought of this fact, allow me once more to emphasize this is still very much theoretical speculation. The religious concept for these three designs is still the predominantly accepted version.)

Having said that, here are the next new premises for why the designs patterns are being reconsidered. The zig-zag designs are then followed by one or two animal symbols and this pattern is for the most part consistent. On the east coast of the country the "V" logo is followed by a wolf engraving. The wolf is carved into the rock at Inverness Fortress; so it may represented of an overall kingdom. An example of this is the Drosten Stone of St.Vigean. The same is true of the stones found on the west coast where the "Z" logo is followed by a boar carving. The Boar is carved into the stone at Dalriada which was the capital of the Scots when they came to Alba c.100 AD. Thus the new concept is the boar and wolf is symbolic of what major kingdom you are from. The symbols in sets of three are the most interesting for in many cases the third creature is usually a bird. The third carving is believed to be of a personal meaning to the individual. Some feel it may represent personal status or rank. This idea came from the Chinese imperial embroidery silk badge system. In their system the Peacock symbol was a civil official, the Leopard was a military rank, the sitting Dragon was an imperial official and of course the Yellow Dragon with five fingers represented the emperor himself. This is the line of thinking which is being applied to the Picts.

Pictish Animal Carvings

From Roman writings, on the body tattoos they followed the same three symbol pattern as was found on the stone carvings. They were not just putting random designs on themselves. There was sense of order and uniformity. It implies that the Picts had a clear structured order to their society.

Since now it is fully recognised, the Celtic culture was the primary infrastructure to the Pict civilizations the various animal symbols can be hypothesized. The Boar which is engraved at Dunadd the capital of the Dalriada Scots can be recognised as the symbol for leadership. The Wolf carved on the wall at Inverness is known by Celtic tradition to represents protection. If we assume that the wolf is the national symbol of all the Picts it shows they have a very different line of thinking for their leaders. They are here not just rule but to protect their people,. Next is the Salmon a well-recognised symbol for knowledge and wisdom. The Stag is the symbol of hunting. The Horse is the symbol of strength. The Snake is for secret knowledge. The Raven is a symbol of the war goddess Morgan. The Owl is the symbol of the underworld protector of the dead. Thus now you have some idea of what each of the various animals meant to the (Celtic) Picts. It seems it makes a lot more sense when you apply the Celtic symbols to the carving and tattoos.

Another type of stone is the Ogham stones which are found in the hundreds across Scotland. They came to the Picts in the 5th century by Niall of the Nine Hostages of Ireland. These 2 meter high stone columns have no Pictish engravings on them. The only markings on them are notches on their sides representing Gaelic lettering. The words formed are often of people's names and places and not much else. As it is, the Ogham stones do not provide any confirmation to the Pictish design stones.

From medieval writers like the Monk Adomnan who wrote, *The Life of Columba*, we get some additional details on their political infrastructure which proves it was indeed Celtic. At that the top was found to be again an elected king. His chief advisor was a Druid, then the law maker Brehons, the warrior captains, the bards and finally the artisans. This was is readily recognised as a Celtic layout except for the how the king is elected is in this case uniquely Pict. When you look at the ruins of Inverness you find it much the same size as Tara in Ireland. It could hold a population of maybe a thousand but not much more, this tells you like all Celtic kingdoms the central government was small in size. The reason for this is because of their feudal like hostage system. Each of the three provincial kingdoms would supply a royal hostage to the High King to assure loyalty. The hostage was treated with the upmost respect and when the King pasted away a new ceremony of new hostages was once again conducted. When it came to the Romans it was kind of a great set up for there was no great capital to speak of to conquer in the conventional sense. Their political system was spread out throughout the land. Capturing and killing the High King did not have the same impact on the Celts as it did say in ancient Egypt when killing a Pharaoh. For the Celts their fluid leadership system was one their great advantages they had over the Romans.

The disadvantage the Picts perhaps had was in their Celtic frame work of being a disbursed people. A nation of a series of independent provinces with no continuous central command, made it easy for the Romans to gobble them up one by one. However, it was interesting the Picts who at first glance appear to be exactly the same as all the other Celts, but they don't behave the same. Somehow the Picts operate in much more cohesive manner and as such are able to completely frustrate the Romans and later the Saxons and Viking when they arrive. The secret is found in their uniformity of loyalty principle. The Picts are very serious when it comes to an all nation collaboration effort. The standard Celtic hostage system is the bases for massing an army together, but it does not guarantee a uniformity in leadership. Vercingetorix is our best example of that. When he was waiting for help at Alesia Gaul it was exceptionally slow and with absolutely no coordination. In the end, though the Gaul's outnumbered the Romans they were unable to win the day. This however was not the case with the Picts. They were always uniform and singularly effective. When you read up on Calgacus you learn why. The Picts only selected a leader who "everyone" would completely follow, no questioned asked. It was kind of an unwritten discipline in their way of thinking. Absolute loyalty to the end; so the one thing the Picts had that was similar to the Romans was a single unquestioned leadership. In the world of tactics this speaks volumes. When Calgacus gave a command "all" knew it to follow it without question. Then again their real discipline system probably had something to do with it as well. Anyone who was found guilty of disloyalty to their chosen leader meant automatic execution by "knifing". Knifing was a brutal form of tortured death. The accused would be tied down and each tuath leader would cut him with a knife until he was a bleeding corpse. Then in true Celtic tradition he would beheaded. Calgacus likely knew Pictish honour probably went only so far and as such brutal discipline was the added touch needed as safe guard. Over a period of 4 years he had strict control of the Picts in their attacks against Gnaeus Agricola. They only attacked at night and only when the Romans first went to camp. According to

Tacitus the effect was devastating to the Roman Legions. In fact the 9th legion was all but wiped out. Clearly the Pictish system was effective. The fame Battle of Nechtans mere in 685 AD we see the same Pictish discipline slaughtering the Angles. It is my own conjecture I feel the Picts stood out from their other Celtic brothers for perhaps they embraced some of the traits of the Urnfield People and this may have been one of them. Later on I will go into more detail on the Pictish warrior for after all to this day he has stood out more than all the warriors and soldiers of his era.

Thus now you have the overall view of the Pictish political infrastructure, their likely ranking tattoo insignia system and from it all how they were far more successful in combat then their Celtic counterparts in southern Briton.

CHAPTER 4

The Warrior People

"Cowards die many times before their deaths;
The valiant never taste of death but once.
Of all the wonders that I yet have heard,
It seems to me most strange that men should fear;
Seeing that death, a necessary end,
Will come when it will come."

WILLIAM SHAKESPEARE – JULIUS CAESAR

Once more it has to be fully established in people's mind that the Picts never referred to themselves as "Picts". Somewhere in 500 AD do we start seeing the natives of the land accepting the term. When the Romans first arrived they were the ones calling the inhabitants as "Pictae" meaning painted people from all the tattoos they had on. The Picts were at this time still very much Celtic and as such referred to themselves by one of the three major nations that existed, Calidonii, Maetae or Vacomagii. Even in this area the Romans got it wrong. The Calidonii were the biggest nations of the three and so if they weren't calling them Picts they were calling them all Calidonian. As you can see the Romans were very lethargic when came to showing any proper respect to the local natives. But since their only purpose was to conquer it is understandable the identity of the people was badly garbled.

Thus finally we can now get into who the northern people of the Briton Island were. Definitely their appearance was distinct from the people, from the rest of the Island and of course following Tacitus writings they behaved differently as well. Agricola knew the moment he was entering this part of the country he had to use a whole new approach in conquering them for they were unique. Had they been the usual Celtic nation when the Romans crossed the Firth (river) of Forth chances are they would have been met by a massive horde of warriors. However, that did not happen. When Agricola rolled into the area all was an eerie quiet. As the Romans hacked through the dense forests they knew they were being watched. It wasn't until they put up their first camp did they now realize who they were fighting. Out of the darkness they sprang and within minutes sliced the heads off of a dozen Roman sentries and then quickly disappeared into the night. This hit and run tactic plague the Romans for the next four years and had a devastating effect on their moral.

So what made the Picts such a unique people to all their counter parts? The Hallstatt Celts in Northern Italy were easily taken over by the Romans a good century earlier; so what made these Briton Hallstatt Celts special. The only answer I can come up with is they adopted some of the Urnfield People's thinking. As such the Picts were a mix of two cultures something entirely unique. It is from this line of thinking I am going to try and explain in more detail.

Archaeological research has found in various bog burials the average Pict had similar dress as all Celts did. They wore woollen cloths with the familiar tartan design on them. A man's dress comprised of a single tunic that went down to his knees. The legs were bare. He had a woollen cape and wore a specially braded hood. In the national museum of Scotland you can find a recreation of the hood on display. Since brooches didn't come to the Picts until well into the 2nd century scholars feel the cape was fasten by a simple straight pin. The women wore a top piece shirt of wool if you can call it that and a full length woolen dress. A knotted cord was used as a belt. As it comes as no surprise there was a warrior class and when he was not fighting he too dressed to accommodate the cold and damp temperatures of the north. He wore a tartan design like pants with a woolen tunic that was covered over with a leather vest. His pants were held up with a strong leather belt. And contrary to the bare feet of what Hollywood continues to show the Picts did have leather shoes. However, not in the way we know shoes. Their shoes were one cut from a single piece of leather. The leather was wrapped over his foot for the proper size and holes were punched for the leather thong laces. As can be seen the common Pict was aware of the cold environment he/she lived in. Only when in combat did they strip down.

It appears from Paul Wagner's book, *The Pictish Warrior*, there was some common sense to fighting nude or near nude in battle. The big one was after battle the Picts found cleaning any open battle wounds was far easier to do. Further not having cloths rub up against the injury prevented infection. It turns out recovery from an injury was much faster than their Roman counterpart. In terms of mobility the Pictish warrior not being burden with heavy armour could move much faster in the field. The Pictish warrior was armed with a small square shield and a long bronze sword that was for the most part an import from Ireland. In the first century there was no evidence of any metallurgy activities in the land. Thus it is obvious just about all the Iron and bronze products was imported from abroad.

In terms of living accommodations once more the country was split in half. On the west coast the average family lived in shale stone bee hive like structure. On the east it was a small circular thatched roof woven stick wall house. Living standards were very basic with a diet that comprised primarily of fish on the west coast and beef on the east. There is no evidence to date that other than animal hides and skins was there any furniture in the homes. Life to say the least was Spartan. Yet considering what was described of the Picts appearance by the Romans they were very muscular and healthy looking. Seeing there is an overabundance of seal bone combs in the museums across Scotland the Picts did have good sense of grooming and hygiene. Unlike in Ireland where Archaeologists have found all sorts of proof that plague was a common in everyday life, the same was not true with the Picts. They clearly had a better sense of cleanliness in their lifestyle.

The economy was predominantly livestock and agriculture. Like all Celtic nations the most prized animal which also acted as currency was cattle. Historians are in general agreement that cattle made up 70% of the economy. The next 15% was pigs. Then foul and chicken coups were about 10% and down in the southwest portion of the country was around 5% grains. Archaeologists found the grain growing was far more extensive in the Neolithic Age but since the Celts came that dwindled down dramatically. Since Mead was a popular drink of the time it is presumed the grain was grown chiefly for that reason. The cattle were a mix of dairy and beef, thus it tells us the diet was not just meat. There may have been cheese products but so far there is no proof of it.

Before I get into the warrior culture of the Picts I am going to continue just a little bit more on their lifestyle. I'll start with the Broch community on the west coast. This was a stone circular fort like set up. There was a large structure in the centre surrounded by a series bee hive like structures around it. From it scholars believe the community operated much the same way as the North American long houses natives did. As previously mentioned the centre building is where the people gathered in making cloths, cooking food and just socializing. Adjacent to the large structure was an underground sub terrain. Here is where they store their food for the winter. On the east coast was of course the thatch roof houses all clustered together, with a woven 3 meters high stick fence around it. These little set ups are commonly known as raths. It would seem there was no common social area for people to gather like in the Brochs, everything was done in each of the homes. As for storing food it was similar to the Brochs but was underneath the house with the entrance being a trapped door on the outside.

Life in general followed the four main seasons of the Celtic Calendar; Samhain, Imbolc, Beltane and Lughnasah. Each of these seasons was started with a major festival that brought whole nation together. As it was from the season festival the rulers had their chance to assess their economy and general political status. This was the part where Tacitus had completely missed in his observation of the Celtic world. It always befuddled him on how the Celts knew when to come together as nation to fight the Romans. He thought they were just a scramble of nomadic tribes with absolutely no connection with one another. Had he taken the time to analyze their society he would have realize where their unity was founded in.

Next there was the religion. I am going to go into more detail later on this but for now I will provide the general outline on it. This subject I find particularly amusing with many historians on the Picts. For the most part they did not do a proper research into the culture and as such missed the main point altogether. Since there were two distinct groups of people there were equally two different types of religious practices. On the west coast seeing they were predominantly Urnfield the practices all centred on the sun, the moon and their ancestors. The Urnfield People believed the ancestors could be called upon for protection and respect for the sun meant a good harvest. It was basically that simple. For the Hallstatt Picts it was all about Druidism. Here they worshipped a series of Celtic gods like Lugh, Daghda, Danu, Morgan, Bridgit and Cernonus just to mention a few. The stone circles on the west coast were not far from the Brochs. These have been confirmed as burial centres where for the most part the Urnfield Picts cremated their dead. On the east coast people were buried very near the raths as a whole body. The Hallstatt had a similar belief that the spirit of the dead would help protect their homes.

As can be seen the Picts had a good sense of community, economics, religion and political order. They were not the savage barbarians the Romans mistook them to be.

Now at long last the secret to the fame Pictish fighting legend. First their political infrastructure allowed them to mass a large discipline army relatively quickly. Further their system provided they could have a single leader to lead the army without question, something which was not very common with Celts in general. Lastly the Pictish warrior was well trained in the art of fighting. Like the Spartans of Greece, the Picts started training their warriors at a very young age. By the time the youth became a teen he/she was extremely proficient with the sword and shield. And yes, they did not discriminate against women from being an elite warrior. The Romans nicknamed the female warriors as "She Devils".

The training of a Pictish warrior was definitely for a very privileged few. The selection of a warrior came through the fosterage family system that was standard in the Celtic world but with a few special additions. The fosterage system in general for all the Celts across Europe was used to strengthen political alliance between tribes, clans and kingdoms. The Picts it turns out took it one step further. When a child boy or girl was chosen to fostered to another community in it was the training of a warrior in the process. So it was not just the raising a healthy person but also to train a high quality warrior that everyone could take pride in. Thus the family taking in the child knew they had a special responsibility in the raising besides quality care. When returning the child back to his or her natural home they had to be at a certain level of warrior skill. According to the Pictish Chronicles it was called, "The Six Feats of Activity". By the time the child comes of adulthood they have mastered the six great feats. This training included intellectual academics that was provided by the Druids. Thus the warrior not only could fight with exceptional capability but was also able to think strategically. He was as they say and all-rounded soldier.

Details of how the Pictish military system worked have been brought down to us from the *"Three Pictish Chronicles"* written in the 6th century. These remarkable documents combined have given us for the first time just how sophisticated they really were when it came to armed combat. At the first level each of the seven minor kingdoms were required to have ready 685 trained warriors. This meant at the very minimum the Picts had about 4800 combatants they could call upon at any given moment. However, this system had what you might say is a kind of militia army. Every farmer was required to have a battle axe and his own small warrior shield. Historians have estimated that by including farmers to the warrior base they had over 50,000 men and women to call upon. Each of the seven kingdom's army assembled under their tuath Kings. By modern standards it would be seen as a seven brigade groups. The Division Commanders were of course the Kings of the three major kingdoms. They in turn were controlled by a High King. However, having said that, this was not always the case. Calgacus proved that a general could be elected and he instead of the high king would command the field army.

The reason for a field general was simple; the Picts seem to have a real understanding for competence. Though the high King may very well be a good overall leader for the country, however, if there was any doubt to his ability to conduct a war he was quickly put aside for someone who was. They instinctively knew they were a small country and their survival depended on a completely cohesive force. They could not afford any meltdown in the ranks as to what happen to Vercingetorix, Boudicca and Niall of the Nine Hostages. As it was to be seen in their fighting technique they had an extremely cohesive military infrastructure. Again, something that was completely lost in the understanding with Agricola and Tacitus. Now knowing this from the Pict perspective it adds a new dimension to whether or not Mons Graupius really did happen for real. For three years Calgacus and the Picts saw firsthand their hit and run tactics were extremely successful against the Romans. It becomes seriously puzzling as to why at the very last moment they would change their strategy to open combat especially when in the Pictish system a leader could be swiftly replaced on just one defeat.

Now that you realize this in the Pictish military set up when reading Tacitus accounts of Agricola's campaign a lot of it makes sense. Tacitus points out the Picts had a system of operation and the timing was always consistent over the four years Agricola marched into Caledonia. The Picts never attacked the Romans on the march. Second they never fought the Romans in an open field where the Romans could gather in their shield wall formation. The Picts under Calgacus command moved skillfully and with precision. They found the Roman weakness was in setting up camp. Here the Romans after a full days march were tired and let down their guard so they could rest and eat. It was here the Picts would strike fast and for only a brief burst. The tired sentries were an easy pick. By Tacitus' own account, the Roman Legends were being hit on a near daily bases and the size of the legions were dropping in strength. The one time Agricola breaks up his force into three columns is when Calgacus goes after the Ninth legion. Tacitus is unequivocal in his timings of the attack, it happened in the middle of the night. Fighting was desperate throughout the night and using his own words "near fatal" when at the break of day when Agricola showed up in the nick of time. To me near fatal means near wiped out. In fact, at the Battle of Mons Graupius Tacitus describes Agricola main forces as a "Legion"; fully implying the Ninth was no longer big enough to be described as a legion.

Finally look at the infamous battle strictly from the world of science and nothing else. For decades archaeologists have been in search of the battle site and to date they have not found it. There is a number of unproven speculations but that is about it. There are no names anywhere in Scottish history that remotely resembles the name Mons Graupius. Strictly from the Archaeological perspective experts have pretty much come to the same conclusion as Vespasian did that the battle may have indeed been simply made up. When doing the simple math on what Tacitus wrote this too ends up not adding up correctly. Tacitus described the battle that there was one legion the 20th, 3,000 cavalry and 8,000 reserves, a total strength of 16,000. However, that is not possible when it was described the Romans left 500 men at each of the 8 forts they built which comes to 4000 men. Further he describes the legions were taking casualties every day but would not say how many. Working the smallest number, if we are assuming 5 or so Romans killed a day, in the six months of marching season, that is 900 dead or wounded in one year. Over 4 years that is 3600. Add in the troops left off at the forts the likely number missing from the alleged 16,000 is 8,400 in real strength. If that is the case there is no way Agricola was able to have fought some 50,000 Picts. Just working the numbers only the Picts, had they really fought at Mon Graupius, would have easily smashed through the Roman lines. Looking now at all the different scenarios to the battle it really does come down to that it was likely the more of imaginative writing than actual fact. Then of course when everything else can be questioned your still left with the fact Roman Emperor didn't believe it happened either.

CHAPTER 5

Fortresses and Navy of the Picts

*"I am sorry to see you here, but if you had fought
like a man, you needn't be hanged like a dog."*

ANNE BONNY (PIRATE 1782)

his is one of the more interesting subjects of the
Picts which gives a clear idea of the two major cultures that
made up the Picts. One of the best sources I found on this
topic was actually in a small illustrated book by Angus
Konstam called, *Stronghold of the Picts*. Archaeologically
speaking the most prominent evidence of Pict forts come
on the west coast of Scotland. The reason being the forts
were made of stone. On the east coast it is mostly circular
mounds and the remains of Hill forts are all that is left today
to see. There are a few exceptions like Dunbar in the south
central Scotland and Burghead up in the northeast near the
Loch Ness. Burghead in particular was an amazing place

for it was here the Picts had what could be best described as a Naval Base. People can't visualize the Pictish savages as being even capable of building a small boat let alone a huge navy with hundreds of ships. Yet it was all very true. The structures design of these of forts show a clear indication of two distinct people (Urnfield and Celts) who had merged together.

On this topic has also to be mentioned when the Scots (Irish) influence to the fortress building starting in 100 AD. Their fortresses were of course very Celtic but with two updated designs that were also found on the west coast, primarily down in the south west corner of the country. However, the Scot influence you will see serious affect the Pict design style of building and in time the Pictish signature, like their language, began to disappear. The most noted influential fort that was copied across the land was of course Dunadd. Dunadd was the Scot capital of Dal Riada. The fort sits high on a mountain and was physically difficult to approach by its natural barriers. That concept became very popular with the Picts and they began building in the most difficult locations for added protection.

The starting point naturally begins with the Broch, pronounced "Brough" that were first built circa 1500 BC all along the west coast of Scotland. They were definitely built by the Urnfield People when they first arrived. As mentioned before they were not forts as much they were reinforced community centres. Lloyd and Jenny Lang's *History of the Picts* interpretation of things it is all very quite simple what these forts were. They stay with the arguments the stone garrisons were Pict and that is the end of it. To a large extent that is really unfortunate for it is misleading. The people who built the garrisons were not Picts but Urnfield People. Though it may appear to be small point considering the Urnfield People made up what was to become Picts. As such it would be like saying the forts in Canada like Fort York were built by Canadians when in fact they were built by the British. It is something to always keep in mind when learning about this particular subject.

Getting back to the Broch now as previously mentioned the stone forts consisted of two circular structures of stone. Reason for them being built of stone was simply because there were no forests so speak of on the west coast. The best well preserved example of the Urnfield People construction is the Broch of Gurness up in the Orkney Islands. The inner circle has a diameter of about 12 metres. The outer circle wall is roughly 20 metres in diameter. What's interesting is the average thicknesses of the walls are 3 metres thick, as such there wasn't a room for many people. The central circle was a building structure and it was about 6 metres high with a thatched roof. The outer circle was clearly only a wall and the approximately 2 metres high. Between the two are found several smaller circles that archaeologists have fuller recognised as the structures of small homes/house.

Irish expansion of a Pictish Broch

Once more this garrison having only a two-metre-high outside ring wall clearly proves they were not for a military purpose. What the main centre building was used for was a small community cluster. In Ireland they would be regarded as raths. It is estimated that probably two dozen families would resides in these brochs. If there was a local chief to these communities there was no evidence to show for it. Bronze weapons have been found in some of the brochs, but were so few it only leads one to believe they were for either personal protection or hunting. In fact there is no evidence these brochs even had a door on the main entrance, further proving is was not a fort in the conventional sense.

What is also found on the west coast is a similar structure also called a broch but is dated to a much later time is the "Tower Broch". They are dated to around 300 AD and are the first sign of the Irish influence. Archaeologists believe the structure was built on top of an original Urnfield broch. Or as some would say expanded upon. The best well preserved example of this type of broch is the famous Mousa broch on the Shetland Islands. *The Irish Chronicles* clearly state these broch were built by an Irish king named Eochaid (father of Niall of the Nine Hostages). Of course the Scottish historical authorities dismiss this and say they were strictly Pict. They go along with the same thinking as Lloyd and Jenny Lang. Having read up on king Eochaid I am inclined to believe he was the source of these new enhanced structures. I can understand why the Scottish today believe they were Pict when the foundations are dated to a much earlier time.

The Tower Broch, if you look them up on the internet is a massive chimney like structure. They were 13 metres high and 8 metres in diameter at the base. There was a lining about 4 metres away from the outer wall inside and between the two on three levels is where the people made their residences. Kind of like an apartment building. Archaeologists estimate there was about 40 families that resided in these towers. Again by Irish historical sources they were meant to be military garrisons. In some were found metal smith shops so to speak and the casting moulds all looked to be for the purpose of weapons. Were any weapons actually found? The answer is no. You have to get into the history of when the Irish Scots first came to Scotland to know what may have become of the weapons. Irish swords are extremely well made and simply wouldn't be left lying around. If a sword or spear for that matter was recognised to be important to a particular warrior chances are it was buried with him when he died. Or, if it was important to the community by Celtic tradition it would be thrown in a local water source be it a river or lake as an offering to the Gods. Thus not finding weapons in a Tower Broch comes as no surprise.

Crossing the central Grampion Mountain ranges of Scotland to the east side of Scotland you have a totally different series of forts from the west coast. These forts are the ones that Agricola came across in his march into the country. From the design of the forts this is where Tacitus got the misconception that the Picts were just another version of Briton for the fortresses here were very similar in design as what was found in southern Briton. The forts fit the Celtic design to a "T". However, the occupants of them did not.

These forts basically all date to the 5th century BC and they are for the most part the conventional Hill Fort. One of the largest of these hill forts the Romans came across is known as the Clatchard Craig that sits on the Firth of Tay just north of the Firth of Forth. This massive fortress of a complex series of circular walls is 350 metres long and about 200 metres wide. The place was clearly a garrison of an estimated 2,000 inhabitants of the Maetae Picts. What makes this design unique is its palisade wooden walls. Scholars found the design was common to the Hallstatt Celt on the main continent. Here we have probably the clearest proof of the two distinct cultures that grew up together. This type of fort and many like it were found in the dozens all along the east coast. This design fort stayed in practice for some 600 years when the Scot influence began to take over.

The palisade fort consisted for the most part were located on top of a high hill similar in nature as Dunadd was, thus proving the Celtic influence. Next as was the typical Celtic series of circular ring mounds that started small in the core and got larger as you made your way to the farthest ring.

Strewn throughout the core of the garrison was a haphazard manner were a series of circular thatched roof homes. The chief's house was of course slightly larger than the rest and centrally located in the fort. Next there was no communal structure as was common on the west coast. The Celts did not have the same community gathering in their everyday life as did the Urnfield People did. If there was need for a large gathering it was done outside in mass. Following Celtic tradition the massing of the community was for the most part for religious ceremony and seasonal festivals like Samhain (Nov 1). Also, when you look at the size of the fort the gatherings would involve several hundreds if not thousands of people.

The hill fortress clearly indicated a location of a regional chief. Along with these were also found two more distinctly Celtic design forts if you want to call them that. The first one was a rath and the other was crannog. A rath was a small wooden palisade fort with maybe 5-6 small circular thatch roof homes inside its walls. A crannog was the same but on stilts usually located in a centre of a small lake. From the Firth of Forth all the way up to the Loch Ness was hundreds of these little establishments. Once you cross the north of the Ness at Inverness you are back into broch's again.

Historians have long since verified that the second largest of all the Hill Forts was a Craig Padraig at Inverness on the Loch Ness. This fortress was significant because it was the capital of the Picts that dates back to 350 BC. The design here was a 120 metre long 70 metre wide cigar shape mound with again wooden palisades along the ridge. The design was almost an exact carbon copy of the Burghead that was about 25 km down the coastline. Scholars feel the function of Craig Padraig was similar in nature as Tara in

Ireland. Though it was not particular large in daily activities, it swelled to ten times its size during special seasonal festivals like Beltane.

Now we have to address when the Scots arrived in force circa 200 AD. The Scots apparently had adopted many of the building designed concepts of the La Tene Celts in southern Briton. This was possible since there was so much commercial exchange with each other so too came with engineering ideas as well. The Scots up until now had many of their forts were precisely the same as the east coast Celtic Picts; the building influence being Halstatt. However, after 200 AD that all changed. The earth mounds were replaced with a stone wall secured with cross lapping lumber. (See image below) This concept was a common in Celtic Gaul. When Dunadd was being expanded upon the stone wall base was adapted and along its top was a thin weaved-wooden wall that was about1.2 metres high. The fence was just a little higher than a person's waist. The reasoning was so the warriors could throw missiles over it. This building innovation was soon implemented by the Picts, thus the slow disappearance of their own cultural identity. Dunbarton, Graig Padraig, Burghead and the fame Dundurn just east of Dunadd all were reconstructed to take in the new design. This is where some historians get just a little bit confused when they see this. They think the Picts were La Tene Celts and use the premises into other areas such as the language saying the Picts were Brethonic. They couldn't be more wrong. The key here is to carefully go over the archaeological research and calculate the date lines. The Fortress Dundurn is a classic example, here there are three major timelines of the building structure and from them comes three major eras in its history. The first is 500 BC (Hallstatt), 200 AD (Scot) and finally 600AD (Dal Riada

– Scot). In other words the fort has three layers of history to it.

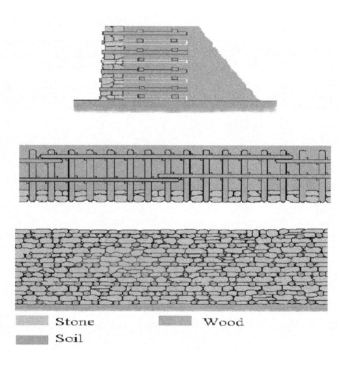

Cross section of a Celtic Fort Wall

With the arrival of the Scots a string of new hill forts emerges and they are all primarily down in the south west corner of the country. Two examples of the era are Tarbet and Dunaverty which are all on the same peninsula as in Dunadd. These forts were all built in the late 300 AD, likely by Niall of the Nine Hostage. When he took over the country for a short 15 years he quickly built a series of garrisons to secure his holdings.

In conclusion you can now see what started as being very simple with the arrival of the Scots, things quickly get very complicated and as such many historians when trying to pin point a single people find it difficult when they examine the various forts and raths. The thing to remember is the Picts as has been said several times now were principally made up from Halstatt Celts and Urnfield People. If you keep that two clear in your mind it should be easy to know everything else is an add-on. This becomes particularly true when the Saxons and the Angles come onto the scene in 400 AD, for things change yet again.

When we start getting in the post Roman age it will be found that of all the forts that existed the most remarkable one that will be mentioned a lot is Burghead. Burghead was the great naval base of the Picts, a remarkable subject in itself. This fortress was built in 100 AD in carbon copy of Craig Padraic however, about 1000 metres long and 700 metres wide. It is located about 20 km north east of Inverness on the ocean coast of the Moray Firth. At its peak in operation circa 400 AD it estimated there were around 400 medium size ships. Thus it comes as no surprise it had an extensive docking array around it. This was how the Picts were able to get around the Roman's Hadrian Wall. The Picts were here allowed to develop trade with the main continent of Europe, in particular with the Saxons in Denmark. Later in 410 AD it was from Burghead the Picts were able to launch their attacks on the east coast of Britain. The Pictish navy was mention numerous times when Vortigern was calling for assistance of the Saxons to fight them in 425 AD. Archaeologists have been for years studying this place and from the enormous wealth of artifacts found they can now measure the success the Picts had against Romans, Britons and later the Saxons in their raids. The place was extremely well built with high stone walls, elaborate gate ways and a military garrison of well over several thousand warriors. When the Vikings attacked it in the 10th century they had considerable problems taking it. Burghead became the symbol of just how sophisticated the Picts had evolved themselves to. When we start to get into the 300 year war of the 7th century Burghead is the centre from which the Picts import goods that make them a society equal to the rest of Europe. The Angle in particular pay dearly in several military disasters when they like the Romans try to dismiss the Picts as nothing more than savages. By the end of the 9th century the Picts are a power equal to any of its time.

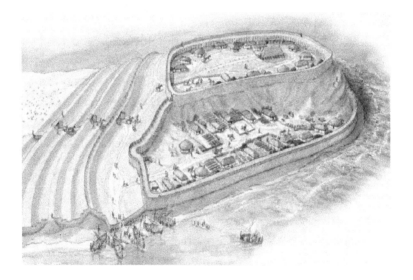

Burghead Fortress

Now that it has been mentioned, we at last come to the Pictish navy. It appears all the evidence points to the fact the subject came up once Hadrian's Wall was being constructed. The Picts did have a thriving economy with the La Tene Britons to the south, particularly with the Selvaes and the Novantae. These two northern Celtic nations had an extensive trade with the Brigantaes to their south or central Britannia. The major trade was tin, bronze, wine and home comfort products such as Celtic brooches. Once Hadrian's Wall was completed all the trade with the south would come to an end. As such it was in 100 AD the construction of the Fortress Burghead was begun. The intention of course was to provide a base for the building a fleet. It is only an academic guess the Picts got their ship building skills from the Saxons. At this time the Picts did have a minor trade going on with them. They exported fish, pigs and dairy products in exchange for metal products in iron like spear heads, pots and cauldrons. The design of the ships is what leads to believe it had to be Saxon and not Scandinavian. Ships were a miniature version of a Viking design but with higher sides to them. They had a single mast and could be rowed with a crew of 40 seamen. The material was primarily yew wood compared to the Irish who made their ships from oak. The Saxons made their ships from pine. As many will know flexible nature of soft wood can absorb the rocking nature of the sea more so than hard wood such as oak and maple.

The Pictish design ship it turns out was superior to the Irish as well. The Irish had two problems with their ships. The first is they needed animal hide to seal the boat from the water whereas the Picts didn't. The Pict somehow knew with an over lapping board technique with animal fat could seal the haul. The other point that the Irish took from the Picts in their design is the Picts had no centre raised platform going down the centre of the ship. As it was they could carry far more cargo than the Irish could. When an Irish ship was loaded with cargo it was often top heavy and in many cases flipped over when a storm came up. From the *Pictish Chronicles* we get the verifying fact of just how large the navy was. It is recorded that circa 400 AD a major storm hit Burghead and with it sank over 200 Pictish ships. Yet despite the loss the Picts still proved to be a powerful naval menace to the Britons as far south as London itself. Clearly it gave the impression the Picts had hundreds of more ships to carry on the war. Lastly where the Picts got their sailor skills can only be surmised was from the Saxons as well. They seem to have learned quickly for it is recorded that by 200 AD they were having an effect on the Roman ships.

Pictish Cargo Ship

Chapter 6

The Pictish Language and Source

My mind is like a train wreck, confused in disarray
I've got thoughts that crash about: drunkenly they sway
Sometimes as I pin one down it ups and slips away
Elusive little devils and the crafty tricks they play.

BABA STEWARTON (SCOTLAND)

PART A – THE LANGUAGE

T he Pictish language is fast losing its mysterious secrets. For the longest time it was felt that this language had disappeared completely when the Scots under Kenneth MacAlpin took over the country circa 850 AD. It turns out from all the recent studies done on the Picts particularly on the fact that the Picts are a mix of Hallstatt Celt and Urnfield

People, the language research is getting more refined. Scholars know the language the Hallstatt Celts spoke was known as Goidelic Gaelic. It is a very rough guttural form of language and it survives in both Ireland and Scotland today. A vast number of historians for the longest time felt the Picts spoke a form of Brethonic Gaelic for it is found primarily in the south of Scotland. To a certain point this is true for the south end of the country was influenced by the La Tene Celts who came to the in 250 BC, about 200 years after the Hallstatt Celts had arrived. Further, the historians for the most part relied heavily on Bede the Venerable 675 AD interpretation of the Pictish language and not taking any other research into consideration. As such since Brethonic is only spoken in the south end of the country it verified the Pictish language actually disappeared, when this was hardly the case at all. Why the Pictish language was difficult to understand is because many of the native language from the Urnfield People were incorporated into it. It is kind of like modern Romanian language it is a mix of Slavic and Latin. Studying the Ogham Stones that started to appear in 300 AD across the land is where they were able to discover the phenomenon in the Pictish language. These stones had on them the names of people and places. It was very easy to distinguish what words were Gaelic and what words were not. In a manner of speaking the Ogham stones have become the Rosetta stones of the language.

In this portion of the story I am going to quickly show some of the latest developments found in the language and hopefully can make it as interesting as possible for I know language studies can be a bit dry. It will be required to have some understanding of this subject for it will help when we, again, get into the post roman era of the Picts.

The first fundamental rule on the Pictish language is there were no written form of it. Neither the Hallstatt part nor the Urnfield part of their culture had any hard copy of the language. It was entirely a spoken language only. With the arrival of the Ogham Stones and what is known of the Goidelic Gaelic were able to at last get some idea what the language was all about. What I am going show some examples of the language distinction from its Celtic counterpart.

One of the recent noted writing of the language was done by a Katherine Forsyth of the University College London. In her book the *Language in Pictland* she gives us one of our first confirmations that the Pict language is indeed made of two different languages and from her studies she has found that a substantial portion of the language is as she puts it is of an indigenous language. According to the Roman historian Ptolemy 168 AD his study of the language claims that 42 % is Celtic. That means if accurate, 48% of the Pictish language was native. This probably accounts why Bede who did not know the language (and Gaelic for that matter) thought it was a language onto itself. Only that the language had enough foreign words in it people like St. Columba who came over to Scotland in the 6th century had difficulty understanding the Picts. However, what is great about this is the fact that the well-known Goidelic words can be picked out of the language. What is left is likely to be that of the original words of the Urnfield People. One quick example of this is the word "Aber" in the word "Abernethy", a place name in Scotland. This word is for the most part is recognized as an indigenous word from the Urnfield Age. "Aber", means "river mouth". It's generally accepted that all the names of places and water bodies are indigenous.

Since I am going to be mentioning the Ogham Stones a fair bit as one of the principle sources for the Pictish language I figure I will quickly describe what they are. Ogham stones (pronounced either; "awgum" or "oo-amm") came into existence in southern Ireland in the late 300 AD. These were stone columns about 2 meters high with notches on the edge of them. The notches represented letters. You read the notches from the bottom of the column up. It would appear that the great warrior Niall of the Nine Hostages is the one who introduced the stones to the Picts. They were used primarily for the purpose of naming places and people. Later when Christianity came to the Picts they got an additional use as becoming headstones to grave sites. What was great about this era was we now had Latin on the stones as well and it verified the Pictish language. The most recent count of Ogham Stones in Scotland are still standing in modern day is over 100. That is a substantial number to be used to reference from in determining the languages. What these stones in Scotland show is when they were introduced the language written on them was all Goidelic Gaelic. Since the stones are found in the south of the country it leads one to believe the Irish believed the essential language spoken in the land was indeed similar to their own. It is another verifying point to what the Picts actually spoke.

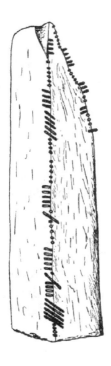

Ogham Column

Here is an interesting preliminary look at what many scholars have now acknowledged to be a distinctly indigenous words of the Pictish language, fully implying they are probably Urnfield People's words dating back 1500 BC:

Word	Meaning
ARRAN	**Peaked island**
ISLAY	**Inner Island**
TIREE	**Streaming**
MULL	**Peninsula**

RUM	**Wide Island**
UIST	**Dwelling**
LEWIS	**Broch – meaning fortress**
UNST	**(unconfirmed) unseated**
YELL	**Small town**

What is incredible with this is the fact we now have words of a near prehistoric language never before known until just recently. Should the day the language be fully unveiled it will mean for the first time we know what the people spoke who made Stonehenge. Again, these words are what were found on the Ogham Stones.

Apparently there was an attempt by the Irish to translate accurately the Pictish words on the Ogham Stones. Words that did not have a Gaelic translation a carved illustration was done instead. This was particularly so in the cases in the naming of birds. The Picts had a certain species of birds that did not have in Ireland so the Irish simply did an illustration of them. Unfortunately their actual names did not survive as a result of this practice. On this same kind of note is where the Brethonic Gaelic mixed in with the Goidelic Gaelic in the south. The various meanings of words get more obscure even more. As such the further north you go in Scotland the indigenous words are more readily recognized because there are no other language overlaps. Except for one exception, that one is very easy to recognize and that being the Danish language that came to Scotland during the Viking Era.

Here is another interesting sample of what they also to know to be words of the indigenous population and that is names of people. Here is an example of a number of Pictish kings that do not have any Gaelic similarities to:

King	Death
VIPOIG	**312 AD**
CANUTULACHANIA	**342 AD**
VURADECH	**346 AD**
GAIRNAIT	**387 AD**
TALARG	**412 AD**
DREST	**452 AD**

Compare these names with that of their Irish counter parts:

King	Death
CORMAC MAC AIRT	**244 AD**
EOCHAID GONNET	**246 AD**
FIACHA STROIPTINE	**306 AD**
COLLA VAIS	**310 AD**
EOCHAID MUGMEDON	**351 AD**
NIALL NOIGIALLACH	**395 AD**

The thing you will notice right off the bat between the two sets of names is the Pictish names are all singular. This is because as mentioned earlier, the kings come from a matriarchal system and their father is unknown. Their last names were not part of their title. Everyone knew the fathers name was an appointed name not a biological name. When it came to the Irish names, the names are in the standard two parts. This is because here we have our first examples that the first name is the son of the last name indicating father or family heritage. For scholars this was a very important feature to recognise in order to be certain the name is Pictish and not Celtic.

Now to take a quick look at Brythonic names from Wales to clearly see the difference of all three and to verify that the Picts were not Brythonic as many historians (not scholars) feel was the case. Since at the time when the Picts were in existence, Wales was divided into about 5 major kingdoms I will take examples from the Kingdom of Gwynedd. All the other Welsh kingdoms are pretty much the same as this one:

King	Death
CUNEDDA WLEDIG	**460 AD**
EIONION ap CUNEDDA	**480 AD**
CADWALLON ap EIONION	**534 AD**
RHUN ap MAELGWIN	**580 AD**
BELL ap RHUN	**599 AD**

Without any knowledge of whom the people were it is readily recognized the Welsh system is a standard royal linage system. The heir to the king is the next on the throne. There is an easy pattern to be seen in their name arrangement. So now when you compare all three you can easily distinguish the different cultures. With the Picts there are no parent/father sub names to the first, it's just the one name and no other. For the Irish their kings are elected the same as the Picts however, it is important to note the father of the first name distinctly recognized to the completion of the names. And finally the Welsh "ap" as can be seen means in Brythonic Gaelic "son". Their system is the clearest of them all, only the legitimate son of the current king is allowed to succeed to the throne. Thus proving in the names alone the Picts were not Brythonic in any sense of the meaning.

Moving along here are a series of words that some non-academic sources say are definitely Pict/Urnfield words:

Word	Definition	Word (repeat)	Definition
Volas	Bay	Arran	Peaked Island
Viruedrum	Peninsula	Islay	Inner Island
Itis	River	Tiree	Streaming
Verar	Estuary	Mull	Peninsula
Tuesis	Town	Rum	Wide Island
Loxa	Crocket	Uist	Dwelling
Pit	Farm	Lewis	Broch (residence)
Mag	Son	Unst	unseated
Fife	Small flute Instrument	Yell	small town

Word	Definition
Tad	Father
Mam	Mother
Plac	Girl

Llawe	Boy
Mabb	Son
Altar	Parent
Rid	Free

The thing now to do is to compare the various known Gaelic words to see if the above words are likely to be genuine.

Here are some Pict words that were recorded by the Greek writer Claudius Ptolemaras in the mid-2nd century. Be aware the words are claimed to be latinised on account he was not recording accurately what he was hearing. Still the root of the word is probably very close to what was actually said.

Word	Definition
Dumma	Island
Caerini	Tribe
Volas	Island
Nabaras	River
Tarvedum	Peninsulas
Lugi	Tribe (Hallstatt Celtic Pict)
Varar	Estuary
Iltas	River
Tuesis	Town/village
Nepos	Two brothers

Once more we now do some comparing some of the similar

words and meanings from recent research with that of ancient Greek records.

Modern research	Definition	Ptolemaras	Definition
Volas	*Bay*	**Volas**	*Island*
Viruedrum	*Peninsula*	**Tarvedum**	*Peninsula*
Iltas	*River*	**Nebaras**	*River*
Tueis	*Town*	**Tueis**	*Town*
Verar	*Estuary*	**Varar**	*Estuary*

Of course when comparing some of the words it is not unfair to think that maybe modern research included some of Ptolemaras interpretation. Modern writers don't give full details to where they got their words; so it is not known how they came up with the words they feel are definitely Pict. So to some degree of caution is advised when examining this example. Using some of the words above compare them with modern Scottish-Gaelic and see if the research is similar.

Word	Scottish	Pict	Ptolemaras
Town	*Dun-Tbillis*	*Tueis*	*Tueis*
River	*Abhainn*	*Iltas*	*Nebaras*
Island	*Innis-Tile*	*Volas*	*Volas*
Tribe	*Treudbh*	*Lugi*	*-*
Estuary	*Inver*	*Verar*	*Verar*

Bay	*Bagh-linne*	*Volas*	*Volas*
Farm	*Tog*	*Pit*	-

Examining the list it would appear that the only word that came down through the centuries that could possibly be truly Pictish is word for "estuary". The modern Gaelic Scottish is "Inver" and ancient Pict is "Verar". Now what I don't have for you is the pronunciation, is the "V" in Verar. The "H' is silent in the word "Hola" is in modern Spanish. If so we have at least one match. Thus this gives a very small credibility that at least we have one word that could be verifiably Pict.

The real acid test is now progressing to Irish Gaelic. This language scholars know for sure is the origins of the Hallstatt Gaelic. Thus the test here is to find if the Pict words are unique onto themselves or are indeed are in fact Gaelic. Once more you have to be reminded on how the Hallstatt Celts came to the British Isles circa 450 BC. They first came into Britain moved up into Scotland and then migrated into Ireland. The Brythonic Celts came to Britain in 250 BC and did not make it into either Scotland or Ireland. Also, in 380 AD the Irish migrated into Scotland and politically took over the country completely by 800 AD. As it is scholars feel Scottish Gaelic is just another version of Irish Gaelic. Using the same examples as before we shall see just accurate the academic observation is and more importantly verifies at least a few of the words being Pict.

Word	Irish	Scottish	Pictish	Ptolemaras
River	*Abhainn*	*Abrainn*	*Iltas*	*Nebaras*

Town	Baille	Dun-Tbillis	Tueis	Tueis
Estuary	Inbhear	Inver	Verar	Verar
Bay	Ba'	Bagh-Linne	Volas	Volas
Farm	Feirme	tag	Pit	-
Girl	Cailinn	Caileag	-	-
Island	Ailean	innis-Tile	Volas	Volas

As can be seen we can have our clearest example to the likeliest truth to the research known thus far of the Pictish language. Modern Scottish and modern Irish have a lot of similarities. It gives ample proof how much of the Irish vocabulary is prevalent in the Scottish language. Also, coming back to the word "estuary" which is very interesting to note. From my limited knowledge of Irish I am pretty certain the Gaelic word "Inbhear" the "b" is silent. Thus the pronunciation is "Inn-ear". This may mean that Pict, word if it legitimate, was in its origins Hallstatt and not Urnfield. However, in many of the other words like, island, bay, river and town, these words do not have a source what so ever in the Hallstatt Gaelic. Therefore, it would not be unfair to claim they are indeed Pictish with its foundation in Urnfield.

Now there is still one more step to take to verify the scholars who lay claim that the Pictish language was part Brythonic in its origins. The two languages that have evolved from the Brythonic Gaelic today are Welsh and Cornish. Therefore again using the same words as above we can now see how legitimate that claim is.

Word	Welsh Irish	Scottish	Pictish	Ptolemaras
River	Afon	Abhain	Abhain	Iltas
Town	Tref	Baille	Dun-Tbillis	Tues
Estuary	Aber	Inbhear	Inver	Verar
Bay	Bae	Ba'	Bagh-linne	Volas
Farm	Fferm	Feirme	Tog	-
Girl	Merch	Cailinn	Caileag	-
Island	Ynis	Oilean	Innis-tile	Volas

Some Brythonic words definitely are similar to their Hallstatt counterpart and this is not entirely surprising, when you consider both languages have the same origins. Both languages come from the Swiss and Austrian Alps. Has to be remembered the Brythonic language only had about 200 years to develop and so it is easily recognized, that many of the Hallstatt words would survive in the Brythonic language. The obvious example in the above list is the word for "estuary". It is more than likely the Welsh word "Aber' the "b" is silent. Thus the pronunciation is "aa-er". That fall nicely with "In-ear", 'inver" and "verar' (likely pronounced "e-rar". As such all four words are almost exactly identical. However, going from Brythonic Welsh to Hallstatt Scottish is for the most part no comparison what so ever. Thus those claiming that Pictish language is in part a version of Brythonic Gaelic is an obvious gross miscalculation altogether.

Part B – The Source

I am sure many would have felt I should have done the source first, then the language. However, when you see what is revealed in how the language was discovered it will be found having an idea of the language first the source to it comes a lot easier.

The Pictish language discovery had principally two sources of discovery and they were in the verbal known names of places and the second from the Ogham Stones the Irish erected in Scotland during the 5th century. Some I have found feel the language is also found in their art work and logo designs. I dispute the first option because I do have an in depth knowledge to the Pict art form and it is for the most part pure Celtic. Celtic art does not convey anything in language like the way the Egyptians did in their hieroglyphics. Celtic design was purely representable imagery art. There was no communication of language in it what's-so-ever.

From the verbal side of things this one is fairly easy to figure out in a number of cases. For example the most widely known verbal description of a location is none other than "Inverness". This is a geographical location up in the north east side of the country. From the earliest records this name has never changed. It is solidly recognised as being Pictish. "Dun" as in the fortress Dunbar is undisputedly Gaelic. Using these two examples scholars have their foundation from which to begin their first catalogue of what is Celtic and what is Pict. The name of places and where they are located provides ample proof of the meaning of what the word is. The word "Inver" always seems to be a word used when near an estuary or a bay of water. When asking the local inhabitants what the word means and they say "estuary' it comes very natural to believe that is what the word represents. As can be told then all the other words that do not have any Celtic similarity to them the process continues. Like "river", "altas". This word is found to be used always around where there is a river flowing. Thus again, it is easy to assume that is what the word means. So this part is not very hard to comprehend how the language now has its first source of origins.

Then next, as mentioned, was the Ogham Stones. These are stones not more than 2 metres high and they are not to be confused with the Urnfield People's columns that are on average 4 metres high and often in a circle formation, like Stonehenge. The Ogham Stones were first developed in Ireland circa 375 AD. The columns have on the edge of them a series of notches. The notches represent an actual language in this case Goidelic Gaelic, the language the Irish were speaking at the time. The columns were used for two purposes, naming places and naming kings. It was thus are first hard proof of the Pictish places and their Pictish kings. The Irish didn't try to translate the Pictish words into a Gaelic interpretation as the Romans did. For Example the Picts referred to themselves by their tribal nations, they did not have a word to represent all the people of Scotland. However, the Romans did. They addressed all the people of Scotland as "Pictae" and when you read their documents like that of Tacitus they don't call the aboriginals by their tribal names, only by the Roman interpretation. Thus we lose the real understanding of who they were. The Irish on the other hand were not like that. They called the Picts by their nations and everything they encounter exactly as the locals told them. So what you see written in Gaelic lettering is the precise word of what the Irish carvers were told.

What is fantastic about this you now have a written confor-mation to the verbal tradition.

Take the Birmaken Friary Stone. This small Ogham stone is on .4 meters high. The markings on it were carved in 550 AD. The diagram below is what it is seen on it. The Ogham letters read: 'MAQLEAG" The translation is: "..son of Leog.."

From this one example and hundreds more like it language experts were able to determine that the letters "MAQ" is Hallstatt for "son". Today that has been con-verted to "Mac", but the meaning has not changed.

PART C - CELTIC PICT STONES CARVINGS

The stone carvings of the Picts are for the most part Celtic. The only carvings which are uniquely theirs is the "Z" and "V" logo letter carvings. From what can assessed so far the letters seem to represent the Over King's author-ity symbol. When you look at the carvings and how they are ordered, they are always found at the top of a stone. Then below it are the animal figures. The tattoos that are recorded on the Pictish warriors by the Romans are the same pattern that was seen before. It would appear as mentioned before the tattoo art work represents status and authority. As far as written communications from the symbols there is no evidence of it.

Chapter 7

The Pictish Religion

The moon in shadow lay
in solstice's midnight hour.
Distant stars gave off dim light
how feeble seemed their powers.
Dark cloaked Druids skulked about,
They moved from tree to tree
gathering the mistletoe
for their dread ceremony.
Primal terror filled my veins,
the blood borne juice of fear.
What should happen to you and I
if the Priests should find us here?

JOHN F MCCULLAGH

The Pictish religion I have found is another subject many historians seem to get it wrong. The general consensus I have found is the Picts were worshipers of animals and this is because of their stone carving. Many of the stone carvings across modern Scotland have depictions of animals on them but they do not have anything to do with religion but more to do with personal identity and tribal representation. It is kind of like the North American Indians and their animal art works that symbolize their tribal nation like the deer is to the Ojibwa, the hawk is to the Cree and the whale is to the Haida. As such to say the stone carvings are a representation of their beliefs is very misleading.

Again, when it comes to their religion we have to once more review that the Picts are a blend of two cultures, Urnfield and Hallstatt. As such it should not come as a surprise their religion is a combination of two different ideas. For openers the Urnfield People believed in the spirit of their ancestors. Their burials sites were elaborate with their stone circles and their chamber graves. The Hallstatt Celt were of course Celts; so with them it was a belief in a pantheon of gods and goddesses; all closely related to nature. Thus when the Picts emerged as cultural onto themselves their belief was a shared idea. Picts as an example of this, buried their dead very close to their homes and on Imbolc (February 1st) gave a special personal ceremony to them. On the west coast it was found the burial sites pretty much stayed the same, people were buried in special burial grounds like stone circles only a km away from the main community. However, a Celtic trait was now seen in the burials and that was the elaborate stone passage graves were no more. The Picts on both sides of the country had simple grave sites now. A person was buried with a few personal effects and only two or three urns of food and spices to accompany them into the next world. As such it is likely the burial ceremonies were kept simple as well. In the days of the Urnfield People, Stonehenge and others like it clearly proved burial ceremonies was once a very elaborate event. The Hallstatt Celts had a close connection still to its founding people the Scythian Horseman, you know their burial ceremonies were extremely brief. Scythians were a nomad race and never stayed in the same location for any length of time. As such when someone past away they were quickly given a fast burial and then it was time to move on. This as you can tell us the fundamentals of the Pictish people. It does get more elaborate the further we explore the culture.

Using the writings of the 7th century monk Adonman when he was head monk of Iona we find the Celtic religious practices end up suppressing most of the Urnfield part of rituals and traditions. From the Celtic Christian Church's perspective the Pictish religion is seen almost entirely Celt. The biggest evidence to that is the finding of gold torcs, bracelets and swords in the nearby rivers, streams and lakes. It was practice seen all across Celtic Europe and it was also practiced in Scotland. From Saint Columba's accounts of uniquely Celtic traits was recognised in the enormous pantheon of gods and goddesses. Celts believed that there were gods in all things living. Shapeshifting was another one of their religious belief. It was largely due to this point why Celts never built any idols to their Gods as was the practice with Romans and Greeks. The Welsh stories of the Talisman give a pretty good idea of how the Celts believed the gods never stayed in the same form. Knowing this particular point is why the whole notion that the stone carvings of animals being representatives of their gods is simply untrue.

Before we get too far with the Celtic side of the religion, which there is lots to note on, we should take a closer look at the Urnfield first for it would seem particularly through the Druids they had quite a contribution despite the Celtic dominance. As mentioned the Urnfield People put a great deal of emphases on the afterlife. It would seem they had a lot of similarities with that of the Egyptians at the time where everything they did was to prepare for the afterlife. Urnfield burial sites like Stonehenge and Waterhenge up in Norfolk England were enormous burial sites. It took years for these places to be built and the laying of the bodies with an abundance of artefacts was overwhelming. This led scholars to believe the burial customs had to have been elaborate. Further as we know the stone circles were specifically laid out that entrance to them always facing the east. People for the most part were even buried in the same direction as well. Of course the facing of the east was in itself specific too. The east was properly lined up to the spring and winter solstice sun rising and setting. Next the stone numbers to make the lineup perfect was always an uneven number of stones. Stonehenge is the best example to knowing this is true. There is one stone that sits about 500 metres outside the circle on the east side. On the spring solstice, as the sun rises, the shadow from it goes right across the centre of the circle and hits a major stone on the exterior west side. For this phenomenon to occur accurately the stone numbers have to be an uneven number. Once more it proves the elaborate planning that went into the building of the stone monuments. The Urnfield People were clearly a far more complex culture than we give them credit for.

Staying with the theme, Stone circles for a little bit more they were always close to a local community. On the west coast of Scotland it is very easy to see today the remains of how everything was arranged. The community broch was maybe only a few kilometers from a stone circle. The West Mainland Island (Orkney Islands) of the fame Skara Brae archaeological site is the best example of this observation. Skara Brae is a broch community and only 10 kilometres down the road is the Ring of Brodgar.

If Stonehenge in southern England is an example of a typical Urnfield People burial we have a blue print to the set up for the rest of them. The stone circles were not worship centres and this we know from the extensive research done by the famous archaeologist Michael P. Pearson. The stones were the focus point of where the burial site was and that's it. The burials were found on the outside circling perfectly the stones. Not all but for the most part burials were cremations. Sometimes the remains were found in a wooden box or if the person was important a stone box with elaborate carvings on them. On various occasions when bones were found the body was folded in a fetal position. From Pearson's research there is merit to the idea the Urnfield People believed in afterlife spirits protecting the living. In the burial site was often found with two or three urns of wine or mead, food, knives, and jewelry. The chamber burials or passage grave were much the same way, except these site were often crowded with bodies. There did not seem to be the same orderly fashion of burial with circle stone sites. It is from this the belief that as the years went by the orderly and precise a burial ceremony and customs became. However, the last thing to note about the chamber sites is the stone carvings on the inside walls. They were always found to be extensively ornate. When the stone circles arrived this practice was discontinued.

Of course when we talk about the stone circles and the enormous complexity to their construction we can't help but think of the Druids. For it was discovered in the time of Julius Caesar much of the rituals he saw practiced by Druids, were seen near stone circles as well as near water bed. Druids knew about the spring and winter solstices. They knew about the lining up of the stars and from the four main festivals they had an accurate calendar of the year. Caesar surmised the stone circles played a big role in their ritualistic knowledge. It is Caesar who makes the first observation Druids came from Britain and that their institution is several thousand years old. Merit came to this observation in 1943 when a military airport was being built in Anglesey Wales. They accidentally came across an ancient Druid community site. The artifacts found when put to the standard C-14 testing discovered the site was at least 3000 years old. It reinforced the concept that Druids were not Celtic at all but their origins were from the Urnfield Age. When the Celts came to Britain the Druids were assimilated into their culture. As was found in southern France the Druids adjusted their practices to take in many of the Celtic customs. Celts have a greater emphasis on the importance of water than did the Urnfield People. Though they too believed water was very much a main spiritual power to their overall customs.

This is the thing that has to be remembered when it comes to the Druid institution and that being is they survived in many different ages. As such they are often associated with different groups like the Urnfield People, the Celts, medieval England and modern Wales. With so many different affiliations comes an enormous distortion of what they truly represent. Two authors I have found that seem to best address this peculiar point to the issue are, T.D. Kendrick in his book, *The Druids* (Senate) and Jean Markle in his book, *Druids* (Traditions and Bears). They both do a reasonable job in demonstrating the origins of the Druids and how they have evolved in time. The survival point of the Druids that was first recognised by Caesar is an overall quality to them and it is from it that we realize much of their practices was directly related to them being sensitive to the people they were serving. In other words the Druids were a reflective historical cultural reference then an influential leading dogma. It is why Archaeologists can now firmly fix a time line to the various periods they existed in.

Now that we have sorted out the Druid part in the culture identity of Picts we can now move to the Celts and how they revived the religious practices starting in 500 BC. As mentioned the Celts had gods and goodness such like Cernonus, the god of the wild. He is probably a good source to start with because he is an excellent example to the overall belief the Celts had in nature. It has to be remembered that 2000 years ago Europe, Britain and Scotland was heavily forested. The trees were enormous and extremely intimidating to a superstitious people like the Celts. Thus it should not come surprising their pantheon of gods were all of nature. Manannam was the God of the ocean and the underworld. He played an important role when it came to giving sacrifices to the water. Epona was the goddess of the horse. In the Scythian makeup of the Hallstatt Celt she was extremely important for everyone wanted to have a strong horse to ride. Then there was Brigid. She was the Goddess of good health and plenty. She is celebrated on Imbolc because if there was ever a time when the Celts were most exposed to the elements it was in February. The Celts were confined to small thatched roof dwellings and this is when they would realize if they had stored enough food. If sickness, disease and starvation were to happen this was the time it would. Brigid got a lot of attention at this time of year. Then there is the powerful Morgan the raven of war. Celts before battle looked for this bird to see if there was good fortune to come their way.

Understanding the Druids opens up many of the standard cultural and religious practices of the Picts. For openers, the Picts had four main festivals each year and they were: Samhain, Imbolc, Beltane and Lughnasadh. The God Lugh was the chief of all the Celtic gods and he was often symbolized with the torc around the neck. However, not too many Picts were found to being wearing torcs so it understood the female gods like Brigantia were regarded with a much higher esteem. Druids studied the heavens and had a really good sense of time, in fact because they knew how many moons appeared in one year (twelve) they knew precisely when the four seasons were and adjusted the festivals to be accurate within a day or two. For example the one festival we still celebrated today from that era is Samhain or as we call it Halloween. It is celebrate on October 31st.

Of course Druids controlled all religious ceremonies which were for the most part a ceremony of divination. Typical of actually a lot of other religions in this time having an animal or maybe a human sacrifice from the death they were able to foretell a coming event. There are numerous Celtic mythological tales where Druids were asked the future; so it was widely accepted what they foretold as being true. In the political circles this was another unsettling point for a king could lose his throne if it was foretold doom is what his future was to become.

The physical evidence we have of Celtic influence is of course the burial sites. Celts were not interested in the stone circles or the passage graves. They were not interested in an over the top funeral service either. Having been to both

Ireland and Scotland I know having said this it will not be received well by either of their tourist boards. They to this day continuously tell tourist from around the world the stone circles are Celtic when it is a firm fact they are not. Celts as mentioned buried their dead in simple graves and in some cases the most expensive item in the grave may be a sword, but this is the exception rather than the norm. Of course if the Celt was an important person to the community the burial was extreme in pomp and pageantry. The famous Hochdorf Prince in south west Germany is a clear example to this claim. Fully recognised as Hallstatt Celtic King the burial site is nothing short of amazing. The body richly clothed with jewelry was laid on a bronze bed, next to him his chariot, his weapons, urns, food and an assortment of drinking horns on the wall next to the bed. The signature to this grave is there were no stones or markers of any kind to note the location of the burial. The site was so definitely a Hallstatt trademark. This is what they also found to be true with many of the burial sites in eastern Scotland. Archaeologists had to search for the burial sites for there were no indicators as to where any of them were. Mind you there was a reason why the burial was located near or close by the homes.

The Celts believed in reincarnation. When a person died he was instantly reborn into another life form. The thinking was if the person was buried close to his home he would recognise his own relatives when he/she took new form. As it was the Celts had no fear of death what so ever. To the rest of Europe particularly to the Romans and Greeks this was very unsettling especially in battle, for the Celts were well known for their uncanny but ruthless bravery. They believed the human spirit resided in the head and as such to capture another person's spirit they would cut it off in battle and then display it over the doorway of their thatch roof homes. If a Celt did not want to return to the mortal world he/she always had the choice of going to the land of eternal youth -Tirnanog – (pronounced; Tear-na-nog). As can be told there was no hell in the Celtic faith. Everything was bliss; thus the reason for their fearless personality. Again, something either Tacitus or Agricola fully comprehended when they were dealing with the Picts.

CHAPTER 8

The Picts go on the attack

The impediment to action
Advances action.
That which stands in the way
Becomes the way.

MARCUS AURELIUS

You have to admit the two movies, "Centurion", director Neil Marshal and the sequel, if you can call it that, "The Eagle", director, Kevin MacDonald, did a lot to raise attention to the mysterious disappearance of the Roman IX Legion. The legion was formally known as, "Legio IX Hispana". Roman records show that up until 117 AD routine accounts still existed on the legion and that it was stationed at the Roman garrison Eboracum (now York). After that date there is no mention of the legion anymore anywhere in the empire. To say modern historians and archaeologists have been in a determined search for the legion is an understatement. Years of research have produced absolutely nothing. Thus it has easily given way to probably the most fascinating mystery as what truly happened. For Hollywood this is fantastic grounds for making not one but two movies on it and stirring everybody's imagination. Did the Picts really destroy it as the legend now claims it did?

Once more we have to go through the known data to see if in fact the legend of the IXth has any creditability to it. To start off with the most respected writer on the story is a Mr. Theodor Mommsen who from his writings in 1902 won a Noble Peace prize for literature. He claims with absolute certainty the IX Legio Hispania was destroyed by the Picts in 108 AD just south of the Roman garrison of Inchtuthil. Of course as mentioned previously archaeologists have been up and down the Roman road to the garrison searching for evidence to this claim and to date nothing has been found, not even a button. Thus using the most respected source on the subject we draw a blank on hard evidence.

Thus as police investigators would tell us, we now have to rely on circumstantial evidence to find out what may have happen to the legion. Everything else simply is nonexistent. The first hard fact we begin with is of course the Roman records that do exist and clearly state where the Roman legion was last located. As mentioned the records show the legion's last posting is undeniably Britain. Accompanying the records there are stone carvings with the IXth emblem markings found at York that verify it was indeed stationed here in 107 AD. Danish Archaeologists claim they have found a number of token examples of the Legion in Denmark dated in 122 AD. The problem with this observation is Rome did not exist in this part of the world at this time period. So in the initial stage of locating the legion we know where it was last stationed and that being Eboracum Britannia.

Continuing on we have to now have to go to Rome itself. Here another clue is found that could help in establishing the legion's disappearance. It turns out there are three reference sources to look at. The first one is the top level Roman military records that still exist in the national archives on all the Roman legions. Here we find that the records show that routine administration has the legion still functioning, receiving supplies and troops pay right up to 117 AD in Britannia. As everyone knows the pay office is our best source to precisely date events. For let's face it if the legion was anywhere else in the empire these records would clearly have indicated it. As it is they don't. Roman Britannia is the last stop for the IXth. The second source to what happened to the legion is by a Roman writer of the time (156-235 AD) named Cassius Dio. He wrote an extraordinary 80 volume text on the history of the Roman Empire. He doesn't make any specifics to what happen to the legion but he does gives us a clue as to what legions were in Britannia circa 107 AD. By his account the II Legio was stationed in Jeva (Chester, Wales), the XX legio was stationed at Inctithil (southern Scotland) and the IX legio was in Eboracum (Northumbria). So we have a triangle shape of Roman legions guarding the central part of the island. The third major source from which we draw one last clue on what happened to the IXth is a Roman document called *Historia Augusta*. This document centres on the activities of Emperor Hadrian when he was in Britannia in 117 AD. Here it states there was two major rebellions going on at the time. The first one was in the Roman client state of Brigante and the second was up in the northern region where Roman outpost were being continuously attacked by Pictish barbarians. Here it mentions that the Brigante rebellion was a minor skirmish where only a "Vexillato" was sent to squash it. A Vexillato is an *ad hoc* assembly of about a 1000 troops from various garrisons. The rebellion was so insignificant there is only a couple of lines dedicated to the subject. Emperor Hadrian was clearly in no danger with this uprising. However, when it came to the northern barbarian activities the IX Legio is ordered out by Hadrian himself to deal with it. The casualties were stated as being embarrassing large. However, no specific numbers are given. And of course from this source the IX Legio is no longer mentioned except that the emperor is now ordering the XI Legio to come to Britania and the famous wall to be constructed. The records claim it is the emperor's words in that the "Barbarians" (fully implying the Picts) are uncontrollable. Thus strictly using these documented accounts only it clearly points out it was the emperor himself who ordered the IX to quell the northern rebellion. It is interesting that in the very year the emperor orders the legion to go after the Picts, is the very year the Legion suddenly disappears from all Roman records. I may not be an expert in how to investigate a crime but it looks to me that it is pretty convincing that in this case the evidence that Hollywood portrayed is pretty credible.

Based on just this alone I am going to go with the argument the IX Roman Legio was destroyed by the Picts.

Traveling further on in time we now come to Emperor Septimus Severus and his campaign with the Picts between 208-211 AD. From his operations we have some really interesting details that completely confirm many of the mysteries surrounding the Picts fighting capabilities. Our leading source of information comes from the damning accounts by

Cassius Dio. He does not spare the emperor of his massive debacle trying to subdue the Celtic barbarians. First we learn that the implied statements of Hadrian's era of the Pictish raids on Roman outposts was certainly true. Since Hadrian's time the Picts are described as conducting their raids very frequently and with increased audacity. It is estimated the Roman's suffered over the decades in excess of 10,000 casualties. It verifies the Picts were the major threat to the Roman occupation of the north and all the guessing about the Brigante influence about the IXth is shear speculation and nothing more. The Picts were the problem and Rome despite the wall being now completed had no effect on the Picts, They continued their attacks regardless. As it was the Romans marched further north and built the Antonine Wall across from the Firth of Forth. However, though a very intimidating wooden wall it too did not stop the Picts from breaching it. When Emperor Severus comes onto the scene in 208 AD it is well recorded of the Roman frustration with the Picts. Severus who had a glorious reputation subduing his enemies in many other parts of the empire came to Britannia with far too much confidence of continued success.

Emperor Severus arrives on the Island with over 40,000 troops. This is a particular interesting point to note early in the story for this count remains consistent though the Romans end up suffering casualties that exceed the official count. What it clearly implies is Severus was replacing his dead as the campaign carried on.

In his first year of operation he simultaneously does two things. He reinforces Antonine Wall and then just south of it builds a massive 165 acres garrison known as Trimontium Fortress. It is from here he launches his campaign into the heart of Caledonia. There is a footnote, so to speak, that has to be mentioned at this time. A Roman writer named Cassius Dio comments on the campaign and he makes no mentioned of the Caledonians as was the case with Tacitus. All we read about is the Maeatae Picts. From it we have to do a little geography check again of the southern Scotland at the time. The region between modern Edinburgh and the boarder of Northumbria was in ancient times occupied by three Celtic nations and they were, the Celtic Selgovae and the Novantae, and the Pict nation of Maeatae. These three nations were trapped in between the two walls. In addition to this the Antonine Wall actually went right through the centre of the Maeatae nation and it is they who draw Dio's attention. For it is this Pict nation that give the Romans their biggest headache.

By 209 AD Septimus Severus is ready to march. He follows the same route along the eastern coast as did Agricola. Not only does he follow the same route into the Pictish territory but he uses the exact same style of tactics as Agricola did; one day march and then go to camp. He figures he can simply reoccupy the former garrisons along the way. From Dio's account the abandon garrisons are in serious need of repair. No surprise here. As it turns out the emperor spends an enormous amount of time rebuilding the outposts at a staggering cost. For the Picts this is exactly what they were hoping for and it turns out they have an amazing success thwarting the Roman advance.

Once more the Picts don't fight the Romans in open combat. In fact there is never an open fight with the Romans during the entire campaign. There is no Tacitus this time to create another glorious Mon Graupius. The Picts resort to their usual guerilla style fighting with a little added twist this time. Since the Romans had seriously pillaged the region during Agricola's campaign there wasn't much to forage for an army of 40,000 troops. As it was the Romans were forced send out party's to look for food. The Picts deliberately released small herds of sheep or pigs to send the Romans scurrying about. It comes as no surprise that in these scenarios the Romans were often caught outside of their shielded formations. Once floundering about going after the animals the Picts would pounce out from of the trees slaughtering everyone in the forage party. Then of course was the usual night attacks on the garrisons. As typical the attack would last only last long enough to completely cause a bloody confusion and then swiftly disappear into the dark. To say these two tactics were having an impact on Roman moral is an understatement. Yet despite it all Severus kept marching on. The Maeatae had yet another tactic which is believed may have been responsible for Severus's death. The Picts were poisoning the water with the carcasses of dead animals and dysentery breaks out in the ranks. This type fighting goes on for three long grueling years and according to Dio Severus is slowed to a crawl. He only makes half the distance up the east coast compared to Agricola starting at the mouth of the Firth of Forth. The Romans only make it to the present day place of Kair House. For the frustrated legionaries they are actually delighted when news comes Severus has fallen ill (likely dysentery) and he is forced to go back to Eboracum. He leaves his son Carracella in charge to carry on the campaign. No sooner does the emperor leave the front lines when his son quickly calls a halt to the dismal fiasco. In the end Dio is unmerciful in giving full account of how the Romans suffered in the expedition. From Dio's account the Romans had suffered in excess of 50,000 casualties. This is backed up with Severus's own scribes who were meticulous in keeping the records of all the casualties and deaths. Thus it is a fact Severus in the three years of operation he has to replace 125% of his ranks. Emperor Severus ended up dying from his illness and no sooner was his body being sent back to Rome the legions quickly withdrew back to Hadrian's Wall.

It is interesting though that back in Rome the spin doctors were once again back at work. The official records show the campaign was a huge success. And of course numerous modern history writers fly with the same observation when they write of Severus. They of course stay well away from Cassius Dio's writings because it is inconceivable Rome could yet again be humiliated by a disorganized band of barbarians!

From Severus's campaign we get other confirmations on Roman behavior when it came to their legions. If in any way a legion disgraces itself it is quickly expunged from the records. Historians confirmed that following Legions were in Britain at the time of campaign in Caledonia. They were: I, II, III, XX, XXII and the XIV. When the campaign was over the first three legions were quickly sent back to the eastern empire. The XX remained in Britain and there is nothing on the last two in what happened to them. Clearly shows that these legions in Caledonia did not credit themselves well. One historian said that Severus was so furious with his legions he openly scorned them. Thus now when we look back at the IX it is not hard to believe when it was ordered into Caledonia it certainly did not account for itself and as such the Romans quickly removed them from their records.

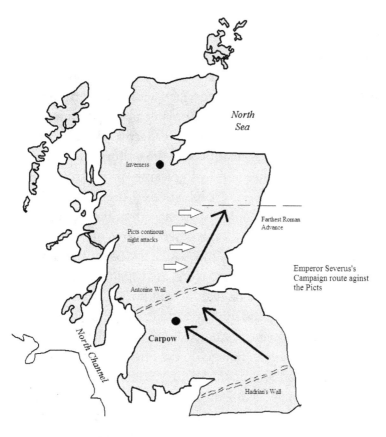

Emperor Severus's Campaign Route

It is interesting it is from Cassius Dio who confirms the Pictish fighting method. It is clear for a people who were designated as the most primitive tribes in Britain they were by far the most successful. They knew right off the bat open confrontation with the Romans was suicide. They learned from fighting Agricola the most successful method was their hit and run guerilla tactics and night attacks. Lastly their determination to fight indefinitely showed well for their quality of soldier. Up until this point in time the Silures down in Wales were the only tribe showed to be the cleverest in fighting the Romans. After Severus that all changed.

It is now important that from this point on that the standard image of the savage Pict is all a modern myth. It was of course started by the Romans and it prevailed with contemporary writers who simply didn't take the time to properly research the truth about the culture. For the story to continue from here on in the frame of thinking should now be the Picts were a sophisticated organized culture, obviously not as technically advanced as the Romans but definitely on par with all the other cultures of the time like the Germans, the Franks, the Gauls, the Saxons and so on. As has been shown they were an organized structured society quite capable of even holding up against the super power of the time the mighty Roman Empire. Like Ireland the Picts were never conquered by the Romans in fact what was happens next is they go on the offensive and now play a major part to the Romans leaving Britannia altogether.

With Hadrian's Wall the Picts soon realized that their standard commercial route with the southern Britons had for the most part been cut off. Like with all societies when their very existence is threatened it was time to adapt or parish. In this case the Picts decided to build a navy. Way up at the north east part of the country at the mouth of the Ness and follow the coast east of Inverness for about 50 km you come to the massive fortress of Burghead. Here is where the Picts built themselves an impressive navy that was actually better in quality than even the Irish. From the *Pictish Chronicles* we learned that by 400 AD the Picts had a navy of well over 500 ships. These ships were similar in design to that of a Viking ship but much smaller. They could only crew about 40 sailors at best. The Picts quickly opened up new trade with the Irish (known as Scots) and with the Saxons in Denmark. Their ships were even recorded as having been in Norway as well where they traded with the Norse. We find from Bede's (672-735 AD) writings that Picts in this area learn quickly to be a naval power in their own right as well. Archaeologists place the approximate date of building to about 100 AD and the naval port goes on till about 800 AD when the Vikings at last destroy it. This port of hundreds of ships has a vital role to play as part of the overall campaign the Picts have against the Romans.

They called it the "Great Conspiracy" of 364-365 AD and it wasn't because it was master minded by the Pict King Talorg. Rebel Roman Legions (mutinied soldiers) joined the Picts in sacking pretty well the whole of Roman Britannia. Again, another piece of brilliant Pictish strategy goes unrecognized. Likely in this case it is even more embarrassing then before. Depending what version you want to take it still comes down to the fact the Romans were completely taken off guard as tens of thousands of Picts, Scots and Saxons devastated northern Gaul and Britannia as it was known to the Romans at the time. King Talorg like his predecessors knew taking on the Romans had to have a well laid out plan if it was going to work. He organized a confederacy with the Scots who at the time was ruled by a man name Crimthann Mac Fidag and the Saxons in Denmark who we don't have the name of the king. It was a simultaneous assault where the Saxons would cross the Rhine into Gaul and attack the shoreline of Kent England, the Scots came down the west coast of Northumbria from Fortress Dunadd and the Picts would go down the east coast of Britannia. According to Roman historians the combined forces were in excess of 100,000. However modern research has shown that number has been greatly exaggerated the real figures were not more than 60,000 total. Romans like to exaggerate as such when they vanquish their foe it is all the more glorious. In this case it was General Theodosius called up by Emperor Valentinian I. Theodosius was a meticulous man so he, to the frustration of the emperor first went after the Saxons and as such the Picts and the Scots enjoyed a good year of pillaging the whole of Britannia. Then with only two Roman regiments he slowly went up the centre of Britannia and scooped up all the loose rebel Roman legions and gradually pushed the Picts and Scots back over Hadrian's Wall. By this time it was fully acknowledged that the Roman economy in Britannia had been completely ruined. For the Picts and Scots had been pushed back to their own boarders the venture proved to be one of the most profitable ones. What has to be remembered that was an incredible operation was the work of the Picts and no one else. Even though Ireland at the time was by far a superior economic and military state they were a subordinate player to the overall campaign.

In 380 AD the Picts were at it again, this time a man by the name of Niall of the Nine Hostages was ruling Ireland. He didn't want to be a bit player to the Picts so he waited and then went about his own operation of attack. He basically followed in the same footsteps as Crimthann and where he was hoping for a better outcome it simply didn't happen. The Roman General Magnus Maximus thwarted this operation as well. Again the Picts and Scots were forced back over the wall. Still the Picts, it seemed were not daunted by how things were turning out again in 388AD they were at it again. Niall was still the ruler of Ireland at this time and now he was definitely out to make a name for himself. According to both oral tradition and the *Irish Chronicles* he tried something different this time. He first attacked Wales and when the Romans chased him out of there he swung around and again came down the west coast of Northumbria. Again it made no difference this time the Roman General Stilicho routed the Picts and Scots. However, what the Picts and Scots noticed this time was the Roman legion presence on the Island had dramatically dwindled in size. By the time Stilicho left Britannia circa 395AD there was only three partial strength legions left. Once Stilicho left the Island taking with him yet another legion the Picts and Scots went all out. Talorg is said was still the King of all the Picts and this time he did not waste any time when with a joint move of land and naval support went screaming down the east coast of Britannia. It is generally agreed that Talorg made it as far as Eboracum (the modern city of York) when he stopped.

Niall on the other hand had a completely different agenda. According to the text; *Annals of the Four Masters,* Niall was out to conquer and not just sack any more. His army swept through Wales when Talorg who wanted him to join him, attacked the Irish settlement in what was to be known a Dal Riata (or Dal Riada) in Scotland. Niall quickly turned around and something Talorg was not prepared for was tricked into surrendering his entire kingdom at a feast. Niall had shown up at the Pictish shores with a small army and invited the King Talorg and his noble men for a Celtic feast prior to battle as was the Celtic custom in those days. Like the famous Saxon Hengist's feast with Vortigern of the Britain's in 425 AD, once everyone was seated the Scot warriors dashed into the tent and capture all of the Pictish noblemen and Talorg himself. Niall offered in exchange for the king's life that the entire Pictish Kingdom becomes a client state of Ireland. Talorg out matched accepted the offer and in one incredible display of brilliance, Pictland was now a province of Ireland. A famous poem is still read to this day of this famous event. Though badly humiliated King Talorg didn't regret it for the Scots dramatically helped expand the Pictish economy and the expansion of their lands. The Pictish territory was now stretched to the very boarders of Norfolk.

According to several different Irish documented sources Niall goes on to conquering just about the whole of Roman Britannia and Britany France when he is cut down by and assassin circa 410 AD. Almost immediately King Talorg breaks off his alliance with the Irish and once more the Picts are on their own. As it was the Pictish lands had been greatly enhanced and for a brief moment the same idea of becoming their own empire when the Saxons come to Briton.

We have heard the name Vortigern already and he stands out in English history for in a way he saves Briton from total annihilation by the Picts and Scots. Vortigern was a crafty warrior out of the Silure territory (now known as Glamorgan) of south east region of Wales. He quickly got a number of the renewed Celtic kings together to form a new confederacy to fight the northern threat. However, as only too many people today know he called upon the Saxon's for help. Once the Saxon's arrived of course the agreement was to drive the Irish and the Picts out of central Britain. As formidable as the Picts and Irish were in combat we know they were no match for the Saxons. Over the next hundred years the Picts were pushed all the way back to their own boarders and then some. A glorious moment in Pictish history had just come to a close.

Chapter 9

The 300 Year War, Part One

I warn you against shedding blood,
indulging in it and making a habit of it,
for blood never sleeps.

Saladin the Great

I call this time the "300 Years War" for that is what it ended up being. It was an extraordinary time in Scottish history. The whole region of northern England and Scotland was in a constant state of fighting. Tim Clarkson in his incredible book, *The Makers of Scotland,* the war it turns out it had nothing to do with the preservation of cultural identity as it was during the Roman times. This was an era of Dark Age Kings trying to simply expand their own territories at the expense of their neighbors. The Angles were at the centre of the conflict, but it soon became clear everyone was in on the fashionable idea. As such you cannot look at this time period of survival but simple brutality at its best. Up until I read Tim Clarkson's book I had for decades felt Bede's writings of the time times as being a rather over the top exaggeration. Now I have a whole new respect for the monk of the 7th century as being quite accurate of what he wrote. Bede is reknown for his writing of *The Ecclesiastical History of the English People*. The book is for the most part all about the Christian development in northern England and Scotland, with a very Roman Catholic perspective. It is clear he was on the side of Rome during the famous Synod of Whitby c.665 AD. It does seem strange he would take such a position when his upbringing was from Iona Celtic Christian monastery. Anyways, what is the big feature of the writing was his massive condemnation of just about all the kings in the region. He didn't see any one of them being better than the other. As far as he was concern they (the northern kings) were all rapists, murderers and defilers of god's law. It would appear from what happened he wasn't far off the mark.

In the 400's it comes as no surprise there was a common enemy of both the Picts and Scots and that was the Anglo Saxons. They had been invited into Briton by Vortigern and they were scooping up all of Northumbria that had been Picts and Scots under Niall and Brude. Further, the once mighty fleets of the two Celtic nations had been dramatically reduced. Saxon ships were bigger and faster than the Picts and Scots and as such were able to do enormous amount of damage. Add in the fact according to the *Pict Chronicles* their fleet had suffered a major setback when a storm near the end of the century had destroyed over a hundred ships in the Burghead Harbour. As it was the Picts were compelled to fight the Angles who were marching north on their land. The Angles it turned out had much the same fighting skills as the Picts and Scots but had better resilience. They could take a punishing battle that ended in a stalemate, but be right back at it the next day. This was a type of fighting the Celts were not familiar with. They would fight for maybe a few days, take a rest and when recuperated return. This uncompromising belligerence of fighting was tiresome and costly in man power. As it was both the Scots and Picts were pushed back to their own boarders. For the Scots it was particularly devastating for they once held more than half of the country at one time and nearly all of it was gone. Dyfed in the south-west corner of Wales and Dal Riata of Scotland was all that was left of their former holdings. Mind you at this part of the story it has to be pointed out Dal Riata had claimed its independence from Ireland. Still they had very strong connections to the homeland.

Before I begin a bit of a geography lesson is required so it can be understood who and where the major players were. The simplicity of the Picts being in the north and the Roman Britons in the south was all abolished. Now you had nearly a dozen petty Kingdoms of five major groups being, Scot, Pict, Welsh, Saxon and Angle. If we start at the top of Scotland and work our way down into Celtic Briton you see the map of the country has seriously changed. It is something I felt was missing in Tim Clarkson's book. He simply gets right into the story and throughout the whole time you are not sure where the places are of what is going on. As it is you are forever looking up maps of Scotland and England to get some sense of place to his story. After a while this becomes tedious and seriously slows down the reading. I think with many people they would simply put the book down because it just a mesh of events. I hope in this fast geography lesson I can correct this point. This way we have so to speak an image of the big picture as we progress. Also, when you discover how many different players are involved in this part I am sure you will be more than glad I took the time in laying out the map.

As mentioned at the top of Scotland you have the Picts. Their territory stretched all the way down to the Firth of Forth on the east coast and on west down to the mouth of the famous Ness. This also includes the Orkney Islands in the far north east of the land. Next you have Dal Riada or as some would call it Del Riada, really doesn't matter they both refer to the same people. Dal Riada was now a small Gaelic kingdom on the west coast starting at the mouth of the Ness and went down the west coast to the Firth of the Clyde. If you look at a map it looks like the nation is hugging around an extended version of a peninsula. From here all the way down to the Roman Hadrian's Wall on the boarder of England was legendary land known as Goddodin. Goddodin became famous from an enormous poem written by a Welsh Taliesin. For the most part the poem is all fictional. Mind you it is fantastic reading. Goddodin came into existence from the merging of the two Celtic nations that resided in the area, the Selgovae and the Novantae. It was really a practical move to address the changing times, but for the poor Celtic Britons they were now a much bigger country they were still no match to the Angles or the Scots. For the next 300 years of fighting they were continuously trampled on until at last disappeared altogether in 700 AD. Continuing south we now have Angle territory starting at Hadrian's Wall. Much as you would think this is a unified region of one people you would be wrong. The Angles like the Saxons fought amongst themselves and as result four minor kingdoms came into existence. For the Scots and Picts this turned out to be a good thing for it dramatically slowed down their advance into the north. What we now know as Northumbria was broken into four kingdoms. On the east side was known as Bernicia, on the west coast was for a short while was a kingdom known as Deira. South of these two Angle kingdoms was might be called a City state that was called Alt Clut. Over time it grew and eventually consumed the whole of Deira. Again moving further south into what was once Brigantae of north central Briton, we have an area scholars still question that if ever it was real, mind you there is more than enough written of the place and that is called Rheged. There are no defining boarders to this kingdom; only that it may have existed. Still further south was the Angle Kingdom of Mercia. Mercia was a power house that simple wanted to be left alone. It turned out that whenever they were threatened they made fast work of their enemies. In the south east end of the Island was a territory that stretched all the way down into Kent and was called East Anglia. This was another very large Angle kingdom that is slow to realize their own strength. Then moving west and into Cornwall you have Sussex and Wessex, where you have all that remains of the Saxons. It would seem that after the battle of Badon in 515 AD a lot of the steam was taken out of the Saxon conquest. Nothing is said much about them until Alfred the Great comes along in the 8th century. Finally we have Wales. Wales was a clearly defined country of four Welsh petty kingdoms of Gwynedd, Gwent, Glamorgan and Powy. Defyd was in their too but at the time still very much part of the Ireland until 700 AD when it finally returned to being Welsh.

4th Century Britain

Oddly enough the largest single state kingdom in the British Islands was Ireland. Ireland you might say was going through what could be best described as post empire withdrawals. In 405 AD Niall of the Nine Hostages had increased the Irish territory to more than twice its size.

Wales, Scotland, Cornwall and Brittany in France were all now part of Ireland, right up to until 435 AD. However, since King Lear at the time of St. Patrick it all began to disintegrate. Brute of the Picts was the first to pull out of the empire. Next Gwynedd fought for independence and then Cornwall collapsed. King Lear found the criticism he received from King Eochaid of Lienster was too much so he marched on him. What a stupid mistake that turned out to be. The national army suffered a horrible defeat at the hands of a provincial king. After this it was all Ireland could do to hold onto its empire. I'm sure for the growing momentum of Christianity this was a good thing. From this point on Ireland becomes an empire of a different nature. This time the Irish is Europe's major centre of the Christian church even more so than Rome. I will later talk more of the incredible development that renews the country of its glory days.

The Northern Briton Conflict

Returning to Briton the focus is now in the north for it is here where events consumed the country for the next three centuries. Since all the countries like Bernicia and Dal Riada were fairly small calling them petty kingdom's is not unfair. The big point is this, in the next 300 years the kingdoms change hands so often you begin to lose track of what is what; so it would be advisable to take notes along the way.

To help you along I made some adjustments to keep the tedious nature of the events to a minimum. I have cut out a lot of smaller internal events from the story. You are not going to see much of when one king is usurped by another. Trust me when I tell you there was lot of that going on. Also I will apologize in advance the names of the various kings are hard to recognize. You have to remember in those days people's names were directly reflective of their ancient culture especial the Angles. There are a lot of Aethelfred, Aethelstan, Aethelfaed and Aethelfrithe in the Angle language. If you are not watching what is going on it may start to get confusing.

The theme to all this fighting was simple greed and land grabs. There was not much in the way of an honourable cause. This new concept all seemed to be centred on when the Anglo Saxon's arrived. They appear to have brought out the very worst in people. Up until the 5th century the Picts were clearly a noble people fighting against the tyranny of the Rome. However, once the Romans left something happened to the Picts. They no longer were simply defending their own lands. Their very image and attitude began to change. The classical tattooed Pict was replaced by a more Dark Age warrior look. Shield got bigger, helmets started to appear as did chain mail, sword became straight blades like the Saxon's and of course the tattoos were gone. Standing on a battlefield with Picts on one side and Angles on the other you would be hard pressed to distinguish who was who. Definitely the calling it the Dark Age is nowhere truer then it was in northern Briton. The whole region as what one unknown monk described was predominantly the colour of blood red.

The Anglo Saxons who had basically replaced the Romans were a Scandinavian looking people. In fact the Saxons spoke an earlier form of Danish. They wore small conical shape helmets, heavy leather jackets sometimes with chain mail, carried large wooden shields, their weapons were either a Viking style axe or a long broad sword. They came to Briton in Viking designed long ships but with no dragon heads and were crewed with over 80 men. From the writings on the Saxon leader Sitric in 490 AD in Wessex the

Angle Saxon method of fighting was simply brute force. They came at you like a mob and were able to fight almost nonstop all day long. Mind you the Picts could do the same; however, the Saxon's unique trait to their style of fighting is they would go at you again the very next day. It was a war of attrition. They took enormous casualties but their natural vicious nature gave them a stamina which was unusual to everyone else. This form of fighting wore out the Britons and Picts alike much sooner. As it was over a period of a hundred years the Anglo Saxon were able to slowly gobble up the whole of what is now England.

After the Battle Badon in 515 AD it could be said was the start of the new age. The Saxons were still focused on the Welsh and Cornish. Over the next hundred years they were relentless in their pursuit west. Luckily for the first time they were stopped at the boarders of Wales. In the north was of course was the Angles. They had taken over Northumbria and Cumbria and were now pressing into Goddodin but here too they were getting stiff residence from the two former Celtic nations of Selgovae and the Novantae. As it was the Angles were stopped at the Hadrian Wall.

A unique change was now happening between two foreign invaders and that was the Angles and the Saxons were no longer allies. Where once the two would cooperate with one another in fighting the Britons that was now gone. The Angles and the Saxons were completely on their own and as we will soon see even now began to fight each other. This break up is to a large extent, is what saved the remaining Celtic Britons from total extinction.

Also there was major natural disaster that occurred in the middle of the 6th century. A volcano on Iceland had erupted and it was so enormous it had changed the weather on the British islands. For over a decade there was a devastating drought going on; so really no one had the capability for any serious fighting. By 580 AD everybody seems to have recovered from the natural disaster. At this time a man by the name of Aeden son of Garain came to the throne of Dal Fiatah. This was a northern province of Dal Riada. Oddly enough it was he who would kick off a new age of fighting. It started with an internal conflict which quickly spread to all of Dal Riada. For reasons not explained Aeden had it in his head he could be another Niall of the Nine Hostages. As it was he was on a mission to renew the glory days of the old Irish empire. Somehow Dal Riada had survived the natural disaster the best and their economy was flourishing. Dal Riada it is said had a fleet of ships that could easily match their parent country of Ireland. Aeden who had successful taken over the country was going to use the navy to begin the new empire. According to the *Ulster Chronicles* Aeden set sail to the Orkney Islands and has little difficulty in conquering them. Like Niall the early success inspires him to go further. He decides to for an all-out invasion of Pictland. King Brude was the King of the Picts and he was no push over. For the next seven long years the Picts and the Scots had it out. It turns out Aeden is winning most of the battles but at a tremendous cost. He finally decides for a truce. King Brude who did not fare well in the war obliges Aeden and formally concedes the Orkney Islands over to Dal Riada.

King Aeden only waits a few years to recover when he's off again on another war. This time he marches south and attacks the Goddodin fortress of Dumbarton and through a bloody siege takes it. Once again the cost is high in casualties. In his siege he had forgotten about another people that were mixed in with the Novantae and Selgovae and that were the Maeatae. These were the people who gave

Emperor Severus the embarrassment of his campaign. Aeden marched into Goddodin only expecting to fight the Celts. Turns out he ran into the Picts as well. The Maeatae changed the outcome of the campaign. As it was Aeden is forced once again to call off the fighting and go home; and with it ended the dream of a second Irish Empire.

I'm sure that in the literary world Aeden would be described as the man who opened Pandora's Box for now the great northern war was on. Aeden's little adventure it turns out was noticed in the south. King Aethelfrithe of Bernicia decides he is now going to take a crack at Goddodin. So the next thing we know Goddodin is for a second time now being invaded by Angles. However, like Aeden, Aethelfrithe doesn't get very far. Goddodin it turns out can still hold its own. Not to be dissuaded Aethelfrithe who is not doing very well on the battlefield comes up with a strategy. He decides a peace arrangement, he will marry the daughter to the Goddodin King (we don't know his name). For what Aethelfrithe was hoping to accomplish in the end the marriage scheme works. Bernicia and Goddodin merge as a joint kingdom. However, it has to be remembered they were joined by mutual political interest they were not a single nation in the conventional sense. Still for Aethelfrithe in his mind he had his foot in the door to ultimately taking all of Goddodin.

Technically the Angles are now inside Celtic territory and this time it is King Aeden of Dal Riada who now notices. So yet again in 603 AD he marches another large army deep in Goddodin. Both the Pictish and Ulster Chronicles give a detailed account of the renewed invasion. On the east side of Scotland just south of the Forth three large armies met at a place called Degasten. Here Aeden, Aethelfrithe and the Goddodin King met. The fighting was nothing short of brutal and went on all day long. Both the Scots and the Celtic warriors took the heaviest casualties and it leads to the suspicion that it was deliberate cunning on Aethelfrithe's part. He is said to have deliberately held back his forces so to scoop up what was left on the battlefield. You could see he still was firmly focused on his own agenda. In the end the Dal Riada's army was forced to withdraw, soon followed by Goddodin. Aethelfrithe whose army had suffered the least in the battle pounced. He quickly moved in taking over both Dal Riada and Goddodin into becoming client states of Bernicia. Aethelfrithe's cunning in one swift move made Bernicia the new power centre of the north. It stays this way till the end of 608 AD when King Aeden dies.

King Eochaid succeeds King Aeden of Dal Riada. He for a good number of years is a client king of Esthelfrith. Aethelfrithe it turns out in his cunning is also a very level headed overlord and does not make any unreasonable demands of client kingdoms. He is well aware to avoid revolt you have to be sensible and for a while his game plan works. For Dal Riada in particular they had been at war for over a decade now and the temporary peace must have been more then welcomed.

Oddly enough the peace that was being enjoyed by Dal Riada and Pictland was not to be shared for Anglo Bernicia. Aethelfrithe now had his eyes to the south; in particular the Angle Kingdom of Mercia. Angles fighting Angles you know this is going to be rough, and it was. Fighting went on for six long years. The Bernicians attacked in the spring of 610 AD and by 616 AD Mercia finally fell. Bernicia was suddenly now the largest kingdom on the Briton Island.

Aethelfrithe is on a roll so he decides he will now attack Chester of Wales. Going after the Welsh is no small decision by a long shot. The Welsh had proven for the last 200 years to be a formidable foe to the Saxons and as such have left them alone. King Aethelfrithe likely had a powerful army from all his newly acquired client states thus felt confident he could take the fortress. There are no accounts as to what happen but the former Roman garrison once known as Isca (modern day Chester) falls to the Bernicians. This it turns out was a notable victory and suddenly now it is Aethelfrithe who the whole Island have their eyes fixed on. The remaining Anglo and Saxon kingdoms all suddenly feel threaten by Aethelfrithe's recent success and it is he who has become the central focus. The other kingdoms figure they had better deal with this king quickly or it is likely he will take all of Briton.

As it was King Redwald of East Anglia is the first to muster a large army and heads straight for the Mercian boarder. Aethelfrithe still in Isca when he gets the news Redwald is coming after him. With no time to lose Aethelfrithe is off to meet the East Angle king. They meet at place called Bawtry. Archaeologists to this day have never found the site but can only assume it was somewhere in central Briton. Similarly when two Angle armies clash it's an all-day desperate battle. Things for the first time go badly for Aethelfrithe and not only does his army gets decimated but he in the end loses his own life. Redwald with no hesitation restores the Mercian Kingdom but also now joins Diera and Bernicia into a single kingdom of course subservient to the East Angles. Diera was another small Anglo Kingdom that sat on the west coast just south of Hadrian's Wall.

At this point the *Pictish Chronicles* are short on the details of Redwald's efforts to consolidate his successes. He had King Edwin sit jointly on the throne with him, in the Northumbrian Kingdom. There are no accounts as to what became of Dal Riada and Goddodin; so it can only be assumed their status remained as before. Eanfrith who was the son of Aethelfrithe flees to the Pictish kingdom when Redwald puts Edwin on the Bernician throne. During his time in exile Eanfrith makes allies with the Saxons and they for their own profit decide to support him in his cause to get back his father's kingdom. When you think about it this is rather strange. Only a few years earlier the Saxon's felt threaten by Aethelfrithe and now they are helping his son to get the throne back. In 624 AD Eanfrith with a sizable Saxon army he invades Northumbria. A major battle takes place just north of Isca which likely means the Saxons came by sea. This kind of small detail is missing throughout the chronicles, so you have to use your common sense as to where everyone is coming from. Since the chronicles no longer mentions the name of Eanfrith from here on in it can only be assumed he did not fare well in regaining the throne for his father. Thus everything in the north once again returned to its former status. A blaze of wars that all amounted to nothing; a pattern that will repeat itself for another two more centuries.

Up until 642 AD things quieted down but of course this only a short reprieve. It doesn't take much to get the old rivalries are at each other's throats again. Strangely enough where should it all begin again none other than in Dal Riada. A king by the named Dumnal felt the Scots have recuperated from their past defeats and it is time to show everyone they are back in the game. He figures he will start things off with a series of raids along the borders of the Picts.

Of course the Picts retaliate to the raids but they find they are no match the fast moving Scots.

Feeling confident with these early successes Dumnal makes his big move and attacks the now Anglo fortress of Dumbarton. This was for the longest time a powerful Scot fortress when it fell into Anglo hands after fighting against Aethelfrithe. I suppose Dumnal thought it is high time it was taken back. Amazingly his siege was successful and sure enough the Angles are outraged. Unwittingly Dal Riada is once more not paying attention to the big picture and surprise they find themselves with two enemies on two fronts.

The Angle response to Dal Riada's retaking of the Dumbarton Fortress is slow on account of a strange internal squabble that happens between the two very small Anglo kingdoms of Diera on the west coast and Alt Clut on the east coast just below Bernicia. In a bizarre turn of events Diera was an overlord state of Alt Clut so the *Saxon Chronicles* state. Something happened and Alt Clut became independent of Diera. The reason was Alt Clut had a clever king named King Owain who somehow not only got Alt Clut its own autonomy but miraculously manage to put Bernicia under his control in the process. This is amazing when you consider Bernicia is five times larger than Alt Clut is. Bernicia was under the rule of the very annoyed King Oswiu who did not like the idea of being subject to a city state to say the least. He of course started making trouble for Owain and it is believed from this conflict that the Angle failed to rescue to Dumbarton. By just sheer size and strength Bernicia should have easily taken care of Alt Clut and then gone on to deal with the Scots at Dumbarton. Unfortunately this did not happen at all. Oswiu found that Owain was more than a handful and an unbelievable amount of time and energy was wasted on what appeared to be a really insignificant dispute. Somewhere in the conflict Oswiu realized he was outgunned by Owain so he went to Mercia for additional political aid and married the Mercian King's daughter. This was another clever move by Oswiu that forced Owain had to stop and reconsider his position. As it was for the time being Bernicia was in a bit of a stalemate with Alt Clut.

In the mean time we have King Penda of Diera who is the only one staying paying attention to the Scot takeover of Dumbarton. Having completely lost his patience with his fellow Anglo Kings he decides he will go it alone and attack the Scots of Dal Riada. The fact that Diera is an incredibly small kingdom compared to Dal Riada it comes as no surprise King's Penda's venture turns into a cruel disaster.

Back in Bernicia Oswiu at long last gets his chance to once and for all confront Owain on the battlefield. This time Owain's crafty ways are overwhelmed by a massive Bernician army. The fight is over even before it begins and in very short order Owain is dethroned and Alt Clut is swiftly put under firm control of Oswiu.

You have to admit it must seem like a bit of a soap opera as one scene ends we are quickly racing off to see how it ends and in this case it is again back to Dal Riada.

King Domnal was watching the amusing events unfolding between Alt Clut and Bernicia and figures he will take full advantage of it. Before we know it a Scot army is marching out of Dal Riada and into Goddodin. However, he only gets half way into the country when he is intercepted and sent packing home. Domnal like his predecessor Aeden miscalculated on the Maeatae. These Picts still have all the same fighting skills as did their fore barriers. Over the centuries not much had changed with them and their fighting capabilities. They still proved to be more than a match in the new age of waging war.

The best detailed source I have found in all the mess that was going on in the mid 7th century is from Tim Clarkson's book, *The Makers of Scotland*. He covers extensively all the warring factors where I am not going to. Thus at this point I am going to quickly state that for the next 20 years northern England and Scotland are a mess of fights. You can now see why Bede was so critical of all the petty kings. The common people were the ones who suffered the worst. Every day there was a strong risk you could be attacked by an invading army.

Not sure what was going on only that King Oswiu returned to be king but in 662 AD, he was now dead of natural causes. He was replaced by a King Ecgfrith. King Dumnal, as was no surprise, found himself in a lengthy civil war in Dal Riada. Of course we cannot forget the Picts. King Talorgan, no relation to the king who had once fought Niall of the Nine Hostages, also passed away. He was replaced by a crafty king known as Brude. So though the characters had changed the conflict remained the same. Oddly enough there was at this time a brief period of calm.

Circa 672 AD King Brude of the Picts has had enough with his kingdom paying tributes to the Bernicians; so out of the blue he stopped. Of course the *Pictish Chronicles* don't explain how in the first place, the Picts were paying the Angles compulsory tributes, but only they decided they were not paying them anymore. To King Ecgfrith of Bernicia this was an outrage. In no time flat Ecgfrith quickly sent an army into the Pictish territory and were tearing up the land as they went. He got about half way into his operations when the Merican's act up. Then he found himself turning a180 degrees and now racing into Mercia. We are not informed what was going on only that Ecgfrith had some very serious problems with the Mercian Angles and had to deal with it quick. It is my guess that the Mercian king wanted to take advantage of the fact Ecgfrith was up in the north and his kingdom in Bernicia was vulnerable. For *the Chronicles* point out the two armies met at the Mercian border and Ecgfrith won the day. Then something no one can explain. Confident from what was a marginal victory over the Mercian's, Ecgfrith decides he wants to invade Ireland and attack the most powerful Ni Neil nation of Ulster. Ecgfrith suddenly starts using ships in his battle plan. Where he got the ships is not explained in *the Chronicles*. In 670 AD Ecgfrith set sail for Ireland. No sooner does he land when an overwhelmingly large Irish army is there to greet him. Seeing the Irish from the days of Niall could easily put in the field some 40,000 men, I would not be surprised that the same thing happened when Ecgfrith arrived. The battle was described as being swift and brutal, not far from the present day city of Belfast. Ecgfrith just barely made it out of there with his life. His army had been more than decimated.

You would think after that incredible disaster Ecgfrith would have figured it's time to lay low, but for him no. He was still furious with the fact King Brude was still not paying him any tributes. Thus in 672 AD Ecgfrith puts together another army and is again on his way into Pictland. King Brude decides to use an old tactic that was very successful on the Romans. He allows the Angles to march deep his into his territory. Somewhere north of Inverness in a valley known as Dunnichen Hill the Picts laid in wait. Just like the 9th Legion when the Angles were walled in by two major forested hills, the Picts pounced. To say it was slaughter is an understatement. Even Ecgfrith was incapable of escaping the carnage.

In 682 AD King Brude dies and he is succeeded by a King Brute. As we know from the Pictish method of electing their kings the two men were not in any way related. First thing the new king does is expelled the Irish out of the Orkney Islands. This was relatively easy because the Scots of Dal Riada were in a state of civil war. As it was The Picts were now solidifying their politics and were once more a powerful kingdom not to be messed with.

This marks more or less the half way point in what I call the "300 Year War". I figure this is a good point to stop and give the reader a moment to take in the intensity of the New Age. However, it is interesting when we once more return to the Picts. Though they have changed in appearance they have kept much of their own culture, especially in their style of combat. From what was a very successful campaign against the Romans is now showing itself to also be true against the Scots from Dal Riada. Unlike the Romans who gave us the specific details into the Pict's success, the Dark Age monks who were writing *The Chronicles* don't. Considering the Scots are being beaten off rather quickly one can only assume it is the same tactics. They draw their enemy in to the depths of their thick forest and once there is no room to move that is when they pounce. We will find later the Angles are the next to learn this unfortunate lesson.

CHAPTER 10

Eight Century of the 300 Year War, Part Two

England hath long been mad, and scarr'd herself;
The brother blindly shed the brother's blood,
The father rashly slaughter'd his own son,
The son, compell'd, been butcher to the sire:
All this divided York and Lancaster,
Divided in their dire division, (5.8.3)

WILLIAM SHAKESPEARE – RICHARD III

he eighth century marks the beginning of the Vikings coming. Oddly enough this does not stop the internal fighting in fact we find there are kings like Kenneth McAlpine who uses the foreign invaders to advance the Scot/Pict cause. What some scholars noted was how anyone survived for with Vikings the fighting gets even more intense. Mind you there are some changes to the political map. Many of the kingdoms are in part now occupied by the Danes or Norsemen, such like Bernicia, Pictland and Ireland. Also, in this part I am going to show a little bit of the internal conflicts of in the small kingdoms for a major political changes starts to take place and from it the "300 Year War" now is in a whole new characteristic.

This part of the story opens up in Dal Riada. In 704 AD the country just went through a fairly lengthy civil war. The country was now in the process of trying to get itself back on its feet economically. The *Pictish Chronicles* point out that despite the country had been badly weakened from the war it did not prevent the idea of going for a Scot Empire for a third time.

Miraculously Dal Riada was able to mass an armada and attack the Angles in Diera. The attack turned into a bloody disaster. The Angles had very little difficulty fending off the Scots. But of course this did not discourage the Scots. A few years later they were at it again and launched yet another attack. This too was met with a horrific defeat. Still not to be dissuaded they launched a third attack in 711AD and it too ended in defeat. With it formally ended any hope of ever renewing the glory days of Niall of the Nine Hostages.

With the failed campaign it should not come as any surprise Dal Riada crumbled into another civil war.

Understanding the civil war will require a brief look at the country's political map.

As mentioned before Dal Riada is a small country located down in the south west corner of what is now Scotland. It is not more than a hundred miles long and maybe a 75 miles wide. This little kingdom was broken into three smaller provincial kingdoms. In the north was Cenél Loarn. In the centre was Cenél n Grabrain and in the south was Cenél Cathbrach. Cenél n Grabrain was the largest of the three and their kings were often the ones being elected to be Ard

Ri (High King) in Dunadd which was the capital of Dal Riada. Population is estimated at around 300,000.

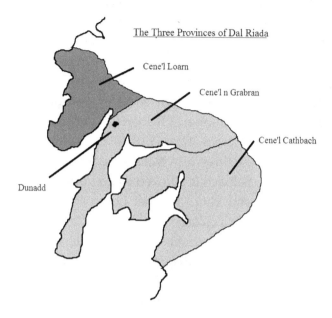

The Three Provinces of Dal Riada

The man who comes to be highlighted in the Scot fighting was King Selbach. He ruled from Cenél Loarn in the north. He to everyone's surprise attacks Cenél n Grabrain and is successful. From here the chronicles now get a little fuzzy on the details. The success is short lived. The deposed king Ainfcellach of Cenél n Grabrain now exiled in Cenél Cathbrach is out for revenge. With a Cenél Cathbrach army he marches into Cenél n Grabrain. Selbach was waiting for him and makes quick work of Ainfcellach. We are not told what becomes of Ainfcellach only that he suddenly disappears from the records. If he died in battle we don't know.

In the meantime Selbach now feels the need to safe guard his holding so he sends his navy of about 150 ships up the bay between Cenél n Grabrain and Cenél Cathbrach and put his ships into harbor on the border of Cathbrach. The king of Cathbrach, Dunchad Bec, is not impressed with Selbach's belligerence and so he sends his navy about 100 ships after him. There is a little bit of a chase around the bay and it looks like Dunchad Bec may have made a blundered in his decision to take on a superior fleet. The two navies meets off the most southern coast of Cathbrach and an amazing surprise happens, Selbach is defeated! Dunchad Bec's terms of victory, turns out to be quite honourable. His terms are the three provincial kingdoms return to their former status. Selbach is allowed to go home to once more rule as provincial king of Cenél Loarn. Thus the second civil war comes to a close.

Of course the honourable ending to the story is simply too good to be true. The disgraced, Selbach is soon replaced by a King Dungal and he demands compensation from Dunchad Bec. Thus once more Dal Riada collapse into yet a third civil war and this one is one the more brutal of the previous two. Dungal's real intentions are out to conquer the other two provinces. As ferocious as Dungal makes the war his successes are only marginal. The other two kingdoms fight him with equal intensity and once more everything is looking to be yet another stalemate.

However, something really interesting happens on one of King Dungal marches in Cenél n Grabrain. He comes across a monastery not far from the border of the Picts. In his attempt to sack the place he runs into a high ranking Pictish official. It is none other than the former king of the Picts King Brude. You see it was not uncommon for former kings and queens to retire to a monastery after their reign. The reasoning for this act is both political and personal protection. Brude it turns out was one such monarch. Dungal recognizing who the former king was immediately and whisks him away back the Cenél Loarn as his prisoner. I am sure his advisors told him this is a dangerous mistake. Once the Picts gets wind of this Dungal is going to have his hands full with a much bigger problem. Dungal ignores the advice and decides to keep the royal prisoner. Lucky for him at the time Pictland was having its own problems and for the time being there was nothing they could do avenge the political insult.

Pictland was indeed rocked in turmoil the country had fallen into its own form of civil war. King Brute had been usurped by a man named Nechtan. This kind of event for the Picts was entirely new. They had crafted probably one of best systems in Briton for selecting their kings so far and for someone to come along and undermine it was an infuriating outrage. For the next 18 years (710 – 728 AD) the country was being ripped apart. Nechtan turns out to be quite the warrior and was able to hold his own in all the turmoil. In the end it is remarkable Nechtan is somehow able to retire his stewardship to a monastery as well and is replaced by King Drust.

Trying to legitimately replace an illegitimate king was of course seen by everyone as a joke and of course the war carries on. Unfortunately Drust is nowhere near the kind of leader Nechtan was and was within a few month of his reign over powered by Oengus son of Fergus. Oengus, which will be explained later, is an Irish import who by sheer force is clearly now in charge. However, it comes as no surprise everybody sees him as an outsider and proclaiming himself king even he realizes this is ridiculous. The times have truly changed. The old ways are now permanently gone. What the Anglo Saxons have brought to Briton is people of strength are the ones who rule now. With less than fifty years away from when the Vikings show up, they are the ones who ratify the new order of leadership. Lineage and heritage is all wiped away and anarchy is now the route to take if you want power.

And of course the biggest problem with this type of methodology is one usurper is soon replaced by yet another. The cycle of violence is now more chaotic than ever before. Oengus who started it all off is of course himself soon muscled out of power by a man named Alpin. Alpin was just another ambitious warrior skilled in battle but had absolutely no redeeming qualities as a ruler. Thus Oengus is able to return to power in 729 AD. To minimize the chaos this time Oengus calls Nechtan out of retirement and restores him as high king but the real power stayed with him. This arrangement wasn't too hard to maintain considering the king was a frail old man. He would soon die of natural causes in 732 AD.

Oengus Mac Fergus, one of the more notable character of Scottish history. As mentioned his origins are Irish from the provincial kingdom of Munster. As such he gets a lot of recognition from a variety of sources like, the *Irish Annals*. The *Annals' of Ulster*, the *Annals' of Tigernach*, the *Picts Annals* and oddly enough the *Welsh Chronicles* as well. You have to admit it is puzzling on how a provincial King from the south end of Irish ends up in Pictland. Some Irish authorities unofficially claim he did it for political ambition but of course there is nothing to support this. Mind you after he takes power there is a lot of evidence to support that claim. One thing is certain his timing of arrival is excellent. Things are in such a mess he is actually welcomed. He is apparently quite astute and realizes if he is to avoid another Alpin quickly set up a puppet government. When Nechtan dies he is somehow able to convince everyone again, he is now the legitimate ruler, but when we learn of his personality he was using more than just a convincing argument. He is fully described as ruthless man and brutality is more the method he really uses to keep the Pictish throne. No doubt he horrified a lot of people as he took over. Having two armies (Irish and Pict) at his disposal opposition must have been pretty small by comparison. Any legitimate challenges to his authority resulted in public execution. Yes the Picts were in a whole New Age when it came to Oengus. By modern standards he was nothing short of "Pictlands" first dictator. The tradition to the crown was now thoroughly wiped out and as such as we will see later Scotland turns into a quagmire of clan rivalries all fighting to be high king.

Oengus now in full control and the civil war abruptly ended focuses his energies on securing the Pictish borders or more to the point start settling a number of external problems, namely the Dal Riada Scots. He is reminded of the disgrace King Dungal of Cenél Loarn had done against the Picts by capturing Prince Brude. So with no hesitation he invades the Dal Riada province and liberates the Pictish prince. The attack was so unbelievably fast and complete King Dungal just barely makes his escape to Ireland. With Cenél Loarn easily taken Oengus now focuses on the rest of Dal Riada and his armies are soon laying siege to the mighty Fortress of Dunadd. It was hard fought but in the end Oengus takes it and by 740 AD Dal Riada is for the first time a client kingdom of the Picts. Mind you it must have been disheartening for in part it was Scotsman's of Ireland fighting Scotsmen of Dal Riada.

Then again another act of treachery occurs from another part of the country and Oengus has an unexpected opportunity drop into his lap. An Angle King Aethelbald of Mercia takes advantage of a temporary power vacuum in Bernicia.

He marches his army against King Eadberht of Bernicia and the kingdom quickly falls. With that move Oengus learns Aethelbalt is similar in character to himself as in that he wants to expand the power of the Mercian kingdom. The two decide to collaborate and invade Strathclyde which is now the new kingdom of the former Goddodin. Coming in on two sides Strathclyde didn't stand a chance. Within a year of fighting when the whole region is completely occupied by two foreign armies. Aethelbalt and Oengus decide they will jointly rule Strathclyde, which is a first in the history of the Dark Age history. Both kings were ambitious and definitely ruthless to achieve their goals, as such it was a really strange to see that the two could actually cooperate. And miraculously the agreement works for a solid 10 years.

Oengus's Territory

It is Oengus who becomes restless first in the joint rule of Strathclyde and so decides to make his move to take it all. He makes friends with King Eadberbt of Bernicia who definitely has an axe to grind with Aethelbalt as such making an alliance with the Picts was more than an agreeable arrangement. No sooner was the alliance secured when Oengus launched a full assault on Alt Clut. Surprised and extremely angered Aethelbalt wasted no time and marched an army in retaliation. The two met at a place called Catchic and the outcome fell to the Picts, and Aethelbalt was now running for his life all the way back to Mercia. Eadberbt seeing Aethelbalt running with his tail between his legs this is the perfect opportunity to even a few scores with the Mercians. He joined Oengus in an all-out invasion of Mercia. On the east coast of Northumbria at the border of Mercia and Bernicia at a place called Newburg-on-tyne near Hexham Oengus and Eadberbt caught up with Aethelbalt. The odds were greatly in favour of the northern armies and it should have been a clean sweep, but Oengus got careless as he flung his forces foolishly at the desperate Mercians. The slaughter was unforgivable and the Mercians crushed the invaders and to their shock and surprise Oengus and Eadberbt were fleeing the field. However, the casualties were so enormous Aethelbalt was in no shape to capitalize in his hard won victory. Aedberbt was once again able to rule his own country as too was Oengus. Oengus who found coming home, the country was again in turmoil spent the remainder of his years putting down one rebellion after another. Oengus died in 756 AD.

In the renewed Pictish internal squabbling Alt Clut naturally finds itself back under Mercian control and generally speaking Northumbria returns to its former status quo. It is interesting when you think about all the fighting that has been going on for the last two centuries it has almost no effect in the area and so you would think everyone would realize just let "bygones be bygones" but obviously this is not the case and there is still another solid century of internal fighting yet to unfold.

CHAPTER 11

The Celtic Christian Church

Nothing is sweeter than the calm of consciousness,
Nothing safer than the purity of soul,
Yet no one can bestow this upon himself,
Because it is the property
The gift of god's grace.

SAINT COLUMBANUS

he Celtic Christian Church is one of the most remarkable events to come out of Scotland. It actually started in Ireland but it was in Iona, Dal Riada where it really took off. The man who has been given the most credit to this particularly unique style church was Saint Columba in 521 AD. The Celtic Christian Church spread quickly across Ireland, Scotland, Northumbria and through central Europe along the Rhine to Bobbio Italy in the 7th Century. The Roman Catholic church found its spread so threatening it started its own movement to counter it. The reason the Celtic Church was so successful in such a short time was it concentrated its efforts with the everyday day people. Unlike the Catholic Church where they spent their efforts in the courts of Kings and Queens. As it was the Catholic Church in its revival after the Dark Ages was moving at much slower rate.

One of the better books I found that goes into remarkable detail on the Celtic Christian Church is Thomas Cahill in his book, *How the Irish Save Civilization*. As it is I am once again only quickly summarizing the events in this chapter.

Had the Celtic Christian Church survived it would definitely have split Europe down the middle. Half of the continent would have been a Celtic heritage style religion where the Vatican so to speak was out of Iona Scotland. And of course the other half would have been the conventional style church we know today with its Vatican being out of Rome Italy.

The Celtic Christian Church had its foundation in the monastic movement that had its origins with Saint Anthony of Alexandria (Egypt) in 350 AD. He had changed the conventional line of thinking of the Catholic Church from a hierarchal structured institution to one of very humble recluse. Typically the Catholic Church which just getting its early footings in Constantinople under Emperor Constantine, I found this to be very threatening. They tried to subvert it but with little success. By 372 AD the Saint Anthony's teachings had reached Gaul and was picked up by another devout man known as Saint Martin of Tours. He seriously promoted the simplistic Christian principles of St. Anthony through monasticism. Monasticism was where a group of people would worship in the same individual recluse principles. Life on a slightly larger scale was still strict, simple and devote. It didn't have much success on the European continent since the Roman Church was already firmly established here. However, in Ireland monasticism took off like a wild fire. Everything that Saint Patrick has set up in the Roman church system was quickly swept away.

The source as to why the Catholic Church could not get a foot hold in Ireland was in the fact it had never been conquered by the Romans. Ireland was still very much an ancient Celtic country. There was no continental control or influences on the Island what so ever. As it was the country was free to develop whatever form of institution it felt like having and in this case monasticism is what took off, but with an interesting Celtic twist.

Literature and art is what highlighted from the monastic movement in the country. Most of Europe by the 5th century was fully developed in written communication however in Ireland this was a major revolutionary development. The Irish were very keen on this subject and wanted to know all about it and how it worked. Under the conventional Catholic Church the Irish found themselves again being restricted from learning the art form just as Ogham was restricted to them by the Druids. The Irish had grown tired of always being disallowed to learning this mysterious form of communication. When it was found that under the monastic system the average person could learn to read and write; of course this institution became extremely popular.

Just to back up a little bit one point has to be recognized the Christian movement in Ireland did not start with Saint Patrick which is the common belief. Saint Ciaran of Saigher, Offaly Ireland is the one who first brought the new religion to the Island circa the 4th century. Considering the fact that Saint Patrick came to Ireland as one of its first Bishops would indicate Ciaran had a considerable success spreading the new faith to the Scots (Irish).

Up until when Saint Finnian of Clonnard arrived in 520 AD Christianity in Ireland moved in the conventional way of the Catholic Church infrastructure with priests and bishops. He would appear to be credited with bringing the monastic movement to Ireland. His humble and endearing approach to the Christian religion is what became appealing to the people and the fact he was willing to share everything including how to read and write. As mentioned it didn't take long for the Irish to abandon the Roman Church and start develop their own. In less than 30 years, nearly all traces of the Catholic Church were gone. All that remained of the Roman Church was found in Armagh (Ulster). Here a cathedral has been built and over the next three centuries the Catholic bishops held firm to holding on to it.

At last we are at the point where the Celtic Christian Monastic Church is formally established. There is no start date to speak of in the conventional sense. All we can go by is that in the middle of the 7th century we find that virtually the whole of Ireland was consumed with monasteries. Be aware that all of them are very much independent of one another. There is no national church order they all follow a similar pattern of operation. The best we can come up with to describe the phenomenon is it was a "movement". Across the land there was over some 50 monasteries predominantly small in size and not having more than 20 in the sects. One example is just outside Kilarney in County Kerry where the ruins of six little stone beehive dwellings still survive to this day. This small little community was typical of the great movement.

Of course some grew to be enormous such as Clonmacnoise on the Shannon River, Bangor in Ulster,

Kells and Kildare on the east coast just north of Dublin. These centres housed well over several thousand monks and visitors. Clonmacnoise turned into a huge international university where students were coming from all over Europe. Archaeologists estimate these centres had great libraries of over 700 books handmade books in them. Some of the surviving books such like the Book of Kells and the Book of Durrow are housed in Trinity College. These books are a testimony to the advance level of achievement that these larger centres had aspired to. They had verified their academic standard was more than competitive to that of the Catholic Church as such was a verifiably a serious threat.

How and when the movement was formally identified as a "church" was of course again a name evolved from an outsider on the main land. It was a situation to how the Picts got their name by the Romans. The monastic movement in Ireland did not have a title for their overall order they like the Celts addressed themselves by the monastery the individual monk came from.

Apparently an overall unification started to evolve with the coming of Saint Columbain 563 AD. He did not intend to unify all the monasteries, it just happened on its own. Saint Columba was an Irish monk who with twelve other monks traveled to an Island on the west coast of Dal Riada and set up a small monastery similar to that in Kilarney. The place was formally named as Iona. However, St, Columba was a very outgoing person and he traveled throughout the land making conversions in the thousands. Many of course wanted to be part of his establishment in Iona and soon the community grew to the same size as Clonmacnoise. Iona it turned out became unique to the other monasteries in that it drew the attention of the local kings like Brude of the Picts. He was baptized by the saint and from it soon lavishly patronization to the monastery. It wasn't long when Iona was the major religious centre in the whole of northern Briton. The Irish monasteries seeing the success of Iona naturally wanted to be associated with it and over the next century had indeed evolved to actually being in membership to it. By 655 AD Iona was recognized as the Holy See of the Celtic Christian Church. The churches influences stretched as far south going into Saxon lands. Great Kings like Alfred the Great and Aethalstan fully recognize the Celtic church in their kingdoms more than they did the Roman church that in Briton was confined to the Saxon province of Kent. Great monks like Columbanus and Saint Cuthbert were identifiably from the Iona Church itself. With them the Celtic Christian Church institution was now fully in place.

In this time another great monastery which had its route with Iona come into existence and grew so large it disassociated itself from its mother church. This was a Northumbrian monastery known as the Lindisfarne. It is located on the east coast of Northumbria about 300 km south of Hadrian's Wall. Saint Cuthbert resided here. It is figures there was over a thousand monks here who hand made some 700 books. The Northumbrian brand of monastery was taking on a more Anglo cultural approach on things where for example the spoken language was not Gaelic but old Scandinavian. As can be told they were appealing to their Anglo patrons. However, the outward appearance of the monks in their brown drab robes, the art style of the manuscripts and the general operations of a strict discipline life was the same as the rest of the monasteries of Celtic Britons and Scots.

A brief statement to the level of education has to be noted at this point. According to Thomas Cahil, the average monk could speak and write three languages, Gaelic, Latin and Greek. Compared to the Catholic Church training of noblemen of mainland Europe; they could speak two languages such as French or German and Latin. From this alone the word went out the Celtic Church education was in fact superior to that of the Roman Church. What becomes embarrassing is the fact a peasant after going to a place like Bangor would in the end be better educated than the noble class was.

The only sacrifice to being allowed to such an advance education was of course the harsh life of the monastery world. Monks lived a strict religious life and everyone was compelled to share in the daily chores of keeping the community functioning. Monks started their day at the break of dawn going to prayer at the little monastic church. Being compelled to pray for hours on end was simply routine. After a humble breakfast but a nutritious one, comprised of whole wheat bread, fish, grapes, mutton and watered down mead. The reason mead was served as a primary drink to all meals was water was too valuable, needed for the crops and milk and was for the most part unsafe to drink. Of course when alcohol is your principle source of drink, problems are bound to surface as a result. We get some details of the extent of the monastic drinking problem that was still very much going on as late as the 17th century with the tragedy that centred around the man Oliver Plunket. He was sent to Ireland to clean up what the church view as the ongoing miss management. He discovered the centre of the problem was of course around their common diet. Tried to put a stop to it but with no success. Moving on. After the monks were sent off to the fields, barns and the ocean where much of the day was spent tending to the common need of the community. When everyone returned at the end of the day they were given a hardy supper of beef stew or roast with lots of bread, fruits and of course more mead. Before going to bed the monks again gathered at the church for their evening prayer. The small stone beehive structures where some still survive to this day is where the monks would bed down for the night. Like a North American native T-pee, all it took was a few candles to keep them relative warm.

The monastery of Clonmacnoise is probably the best preserved Celtic Church of where you can still see evidence of the everyday life of the monastic world. You can go on the internet and see for yourself an enormous amount of pictures of the site and thus get a fuller idea of what it was like. Clonmacnoise was founded by Saint Ciaran in 544 AD. As mentioned it started on humble origins but as time went by it grew in popularity and became one of the leading centres of the Celtic Church. The complex had a variety of rectangular buildings where scribes were hard at work putting great books together and carving beautiful Celtic stone crosses. This was another great feature of the Celtic Church was their stone crosses. These beautiful unique design crosses inside a Celtic Circle was something all their own. The circle was representative of the pagan Celtic god Lugh. Considering when the Christian Church started Ireland was still very much a Celtic country. The Torc around the average person's neck was symbolic to their pagan gods. The church principle was not destroy the old religion but to have its symbols immersed into the new religion. It was an easier way to convert the people to the new religion and thus how we today have the fame of the Celtic cross. As it was with the Celtic Christian Church promoted far more of the Celtic arts then did the Catholic Church and was even further embraced by the populous. The style of art in such great books like the Book of Kells and the Book of Durrow is recognized as Le Tene Celtic. Clonmacnoise has on its ground some of the best examples of this art style in their burial crosses. It shows just how advance the Celtic Christian church had become. Needless to say the cultural development became an obsession where from generous donors the books were laden with expensive stones on their covers. Soon the monasteries like Clonmacnoise got an international reputation as also being place of great wealth. That wealth in time drew the attention of the Vikings.

Page from the Book of Kells

Now that we have idea of what the Celtic church consisted of it and how it became popular with the common people it's time to take a look at some of the great people who promoted their ideals.

Before we can address to the Celtic church in Scotland we have to recognize that the land was like Ireland already for the most part Christian. The two major names that come up are Saint Ninian of Whithorn and Saint Mael-rubha of Abernethy. The only primary source we have of Ninian is from Bedes writings. Unfortunately we have no specific dates of when Ninian first came to the land of the Picts. He is credited as being the very first to bring Christianity to the Picts in the late 4th century. He managed to Christianized many of the Picts in south west Scotland. Mael-rubha was a Celtic monk who came from Derry Ireland and he is credited as Christianizing the Picts in the south east side of the country and Abernethy was his centre of operation in the late part of 6th century. So as it was the Picts got their first real exposure to the Celtic church from Mael-rubha and not Saint Columba. Saint Columba who was already set up in in Iona was primarily concentrating his efforts in his establishment then spreading the faith. It wasn't until he decides to travel to Inverness the Pict capital when everything changes.

Saint Columba though not the founder of the new Celtic Church movement was definitely its biggest promoter and the man who best defined its identity with the rest of Europe. Columba was born in 521 AD in the now county Donegal Ireland. His father was the great grandson of the Niall of the Nine Hostages; so Columba was of noble birth. At an early age he entered the abbey of Clonard on the Boyne River. Here he got his foundation in the new Celtic Christian faith and also learned Latin. He studied under St.

Finian and was formally ordained as a monk there. Then in 560 AD an incident occurred where Columba had copied without permission a psalter owned by St. Finian. What started as a simple quarrel spread to involving other people and eventually up in Sligo a major pitch battle took place where hundreds of people lost their lives. From it a Synod of monks was called and St Columba was threatened with excommunication for his part in the conflict. He decided he would go on a self-exile to Iona, where he took with him twelve monks on the trip.

The Island of Iona was the possession of King Conall mac Comgail of Dal Riada. He gave the Island to the monks to settle. Here for the next three years Columba spread Christianity through the North West part of the Pictish lands. He then decided to travel to Fortriu of Inverness to meet with the Pictish High King Bridei. He won the King over and from now on was able to seriously Christianize to the rest of the Pictish lands in the north. Seeing most of the Pictish lands had been Christianized by Columba, Iona naturally became a more important centre then Whithorn and Abernethy. This is how Iona became the main monastic centre of Scotland. Columba turned into a great literary man as well he ended up writing some 300 books in his time. Unfortunately nearly all of them were later destroyed by the Vikings. Shortly before he died he went back to Durrow Ireland. In 597 AD he passed away in Iona itself.

From here Iona grew rapidly as an intuition onto itself. In 635 AD its influence moved down in Northumbria where the Angles embraced the religion. It was in this time frame the title *Celtic Christianity* began to evolve onto itself. There was no formal naming of the religious practice. People in general call the religion by this name for they knew it was a separate organization to that of the Roman Catholic

Church. By the time of the fame Synod of Whitby in 664 AD the Celtic Christian Church title was fully acknowledged by everyone. Also by this point in time most of the monasteries in Ireland decided to be associated to the new movement as well and as such regarded themselves as very much part of the Iona Institution. As it was the Celtic Christian Church influence was throughout the whole of Scotland, Ireland and Northumbria.

It should be noted at this time the Celtic Christian Church that was in Wales and Cornwall remained defiantly independent of Iona. Though on the surface they looked and practiced all the same principles of the Iona church they swore their loyalties to the monastic order that was started by Saint David of Wales. The decision that came down from the Synod of Whitby to go Roman Catholic was simply ignored by the Welsh Celtic Christian Church. Mind you what is remarkable was the how much of the British Islands followed the Celtic Christian principle verses those who had followed the Roman Catholic Church. What we know as England today was the only part of the Island that was under the Catholic influence and just barely at that. Saint Augustine is regarded as the great saint of the Anglo Saxons people. He was sent by Pope Gregory to promote the Catholic Church in the south. There is far too much credit given the Benedictine monk. King Aethelberht was the overlord ruler of the Angles in Kent and East Anglia. On very limited terms he allowed Augustine the Catholic Church to spread. It was excruciatingly slow and only the south east corner of Britain became Roman Catholic by the time Augustine died in 604 AD. The Catholic influence from 604 to 664 AD just barely manage to spread its influence into Mercia when the big Synod of Whitby took place. Clearly the Celtic Christian Church on the British Island was much larger and far more established then was the Roman Catholic Church.

The Synod of Whitby - the Game Changer -

At the Abbey Hilda of Whitby which is on the east coast of Britain just north east of Manchester is where this famed conference or Synod, took place between the Celtic Christian Church and the Roman Catholic Church. How the Synod came about was from an incident that occurred in Diera. King Alchfrith who was the ruler of the small state evicted from his kingdom the monks of Iona. Of course this caused an outrage in Iona and so they appealed to King Oswy who was the overlord king of Diera which was a client kingdom of Bernicia. King Oswy presided over the hearing. The Iona church had the advantage in this case for Oswy had just recently married an Ui Neil princess of Ulster; so his political leanings from the outset was pro Celtic Church. However, by and large he saw the two churches very similar and was a little bit confused why there was any conflict in the first place.

It turned out the when the Synod got underway they were indeed very similar in just about all their beliefs and practices. It has to be remembered the Catholic Church in Britain was for the most part monastic as well; so they were all in the same monk attire as was the Celtic monks. The only difference was in colour. The Celtic monks wore brown robes while the Catholic Benedictine monks wore black robes. To Oswy more than likely found the two groups to be exactly the same in appearance and would not have entertained any arguments on this point at all. For the Celtic Church the monk Colmán was their chief spokesman and for the Roman Church the monk Wilfred was their leading spokesman.

To Oswy the surprising argument that ended up dominating the Synod was on the day from which Easter was celebrated. Both churches celebrated the event around the time frame of the Jewish religious holiday of Passover. However, it turned out the two institutions were on different calendars and from them two different rules to celebrate Easter on. The Roman Catholic Church was on the Gregorian calendar and Easter is dictated to be celebrated on a Sunday and there is no compromise on this point. The Celtic Christian Church was on the old Julian calendar and their uncompromising rule was Easter is to be celebrated precisely 14 days after the Passover. As it turns out the 14th day often fell on a Monday and that was the day they celebrated Easter.

Arguments were passionate and skillfully present by Wilfred and Colmán as far as Oswy was concerned it was a stalemate; until an unlikely subject emerge which instantly caught the attention of the king. Both parties claimed their origins of heritage was from St Peter the apostle, but the Celtic Church since they were founded by Saint Columba decided they will follow his principles. To Oswy he immediately realized the Celtic Church was simply a church that has decided on their own to practice certain customs like Easter of their own preference. The church that claims to be the followers of Saint Peter of Rome (and that was the crux) should be uniform with the church operating out of Rome. Meaning the Celtic Christian Church was not uniform to its foundation. Oswy was able at this point to draw the Synod to a conclusion and make final decision on the conflict between the two great institutions.

He ruled that the Celtic Christian Church is inconsistent with the norms of the principles to the basic Christian Church teachings. Since they claim they were the followers of Peter the Apostle of Rome then they should be in line with concepts that come out of Rome. In other words the Celtic Catholic Church should unify itself with that of the Roman Catholic Church. The conclusion made by the king took everybody off guard. Here was a major conference to restore the Celtic Christian monks back in Diera and they find out their whole institution should be revamped and submit themselves to the Roman Catholic Church in general. To the Catholic congregation the decision was an achievement beyond all their wildest expectations. Suddenly in a stroke of a pen they were not only to gain the disputed territory of Diera but would in fact consume the whole the Celtic Christian church in the process. I am sure everyone was dumbfounded when they heard the final verdict and not quite sure what to do next. In fact it was a shock to all and for both sides it took decades for that fateful decision to finally sink in.

The two most fame monks Saint Cuthbert and Saint Adonman were the two men whole fully embraced the final decision and promoted that the Celtic Christian Church should indeed enter into the Roman Catholic fold. Iona in 714 AD became Roman Catholic and the Celtic Christian Church formally disappeared into the pages of history.

CHAPTER 12

The Birth of Scotland

Because Cináed with many troops lives no longer
there is weeping in every house,
there is no king of his worth under heaven
as far as the borders of Rome

UNKNOWN - SCOTTISH

Despite the incredible development of the Celtic Christian Church it did nothing to stop or even to slow down all the fighting that was going on in northern Briton. Some authors I read have referred to the "300 Year War" period as the great civil war. Dal Riada, Pictland, Bernicia, Alt Clut, Diera and Mercia continued to raid and invade each other with absolutely no restraint. By the end of the 8th century it was at long was last going to take its toll in a whole new direction.

In 793 AD to be exact, Norse Viking ships appeared off the coast the Lindisfarne abbey. The number of ships was not recorded for it took everybody by surprise. The ships landed and with ruthless precision went into the monastery and slaughtered everyone who could not escape. Then they pillage the grounds of all its wealth. Hard to believe a monastery would have any wealth, but as it turns out they had lots and the Vikings knew it. As it was when they first started their raids they attacked the monasteries first. Over the years the monasteries had grown fat from their wealthy patrons and as such they were extravagant places to plunder. Many of their altar pieces were plated in pure gold and their books were elaborately decorated with expensive stones such as rubies and diamonds. The Vikings were not interested in the Christian religion or the integrity of culture, they melted down the gold and ripped off the rubies from the books and threw the rest into the fire. I personally went to the National Museum of Copenhagen to see if there was anything preserved from the Viking raids from the British monasteries and found there was absolutely nothing. The Lindisfarne Abbey historians agree they had over 700 handmade books and from them only one survived and that was the Lindisfarne Gospel.

In 794 AD Norse ships now appeared off Iona the main centre of the entire Celtic Christian Church. Like Lindisfarne the Vikings ravaged the place and killed nearly everyone and those who were not slaughtered were dragged off into slavery. It would appear after this second attack being unbelievably easy it open the flood gate to attacks all over Briton and all along the east coast of Ireland. The concentration was of course on the undefended monasteries like Kells, Yarrow, Abernethy, Durrow, Clonmacnoise and Bangor, just to mention a few. For the local lords both

Celtic and Anglo Saxon they were virtually helpless for the attacks were so swift and unpredictable they simply could not react to them fast enough.

Depending upon what historian you want to go with the first, serious Viking invasion forces happen circa 835 AD. Some say the first attack was up in the Orkney Islands others says it was down in Kent. I personally support the northern sector first for there is a lot more evidence to support that claim. Tim Clarkson in his book *The Makers of Scotland* has enormous evidence to justify the Vikings began in the north. When it came to the Orkney Islands the Vikings were not in the least bit intimidated from reprisals from the Picts. The Islands were taken in a matter of days and the inhabitants were exterminated. Historians feel even to this day this was the very first example of genocide. The Picts of course did try to counter the onslaught but with humiliating results. The Picts after 300 years of exhaustive internal feuding were simply no match to the well-oiled war machine of the Vikings. From the one and only attempt to retake the Orkney's the Picts quickly realized it was better to simply abandon it. Thus the Islands became permanently Norse for the next 200 years. Needless to say it was a confirmation to the Norse the Britons were inferior fighters to the ruthless invaders. They re-attack the Yarrow Abbey in 837 AD and then they moved inland and swept aside the Bernician armies. Then it was onto Ireland where the Norse established a firm holds on what became known as Dublin. After this it was Wexford, the Island of Man, Derry, Anglesey and Cornwall. The Irish Sea once crowded with Irish ships of Niall of the Nine Hostages was now completely consumed with Viking ships. Up until 840 AD all the attacks were from the Norsemen of Norway, but after this, things get even more chaotic when the Danes from Denmark show up. To a certain extent the Anglo Saxons had some relief for the Danes not only attacked English but also the Norse. Considering they were basically the same type of culture it was in effect a kind of civil war. The Dane's raids were primary in the south east corner of Anglo Briton. After that they swept up into the Irish Sea and sacked Norse ships loaded down with booty and slaves. Historians generally agree the slave market particularly down in Constantinople was now flooded with slaves and the value of the slave market fell dramatically. The island economy was shattered.

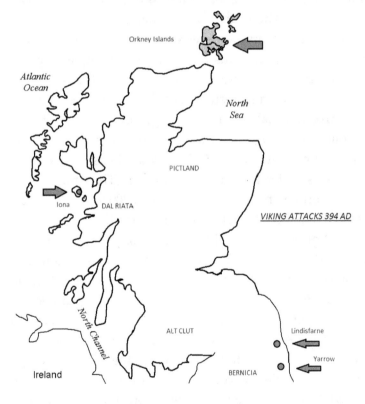

Map of Viking Attacks

In amongst all this chaos a remarkable event begins to unfold. A man named (Cinaed) Kenneth MacAlpin, who is generally recognized as the *first official king* of "Scotland" emerges out of Dal Riada. To be precise he came from the dominant province of Cenél n Grabrain and so with his noble up bringing he was already accustomed to be a front runner. Like all his numerous predecessors Dal Riada's physically small territory compared to his neighbors made no difference to him. The Scots in general were always an equal match to all their rivals be they Picts or Angles.

Circa 843 AD Kenneth becomes the Ard Ri of Dal Riada. He has his eyes firmly fixed on the Picts but he knows he first must deal the Norsemen. When he came to reign Dal Riada like all the surrounding nations were under constant attacks by the Vikings. King Olaf of Dublin was controlling all the raids and invasions of the west coastlines. Kenneth comes up with a brilliant plan to marry off his daughter Mael Muire to the Norse King in order secure a lasting peace. And it works! The Norse leaves Dal Riada alone and free them from attacks for the next 25 years.

The Picts at the time were ruled by an incompetent king named Kenneth son of Ferath. He had been on numerous occasions was humiliated by the Vikings from the Shetlands (Northwest Scotland) and left the Picts exposed to foreign intervention. As such it was easy for Kenneth MacAlpin in 848 AD to take an army and marched into Pictland. For a brief two years the new Pict King Bridei offered a feeble attempt to resist the attack. Frustrated with such a poor defence the Pictish nobles sided with Kenneth MacAlpin and in a snap Pictland was now completely Scot. I'm sure for the Picts it had to be nothing short of amazing. For over a hundred years they tried to do this and the Picts had no difficulty in shattering their dreams. Then Kenneth comes along and just like Niall basically walks in and its over!

From this point on Kenneth began to a program from which he dismantled the Pictish culture. He is not going for the old hostage system as was the standing tradition. He was out to take Pictland over in the sense we today would understand. The Picts were on the road to completely disappear. He started with the Pictish nobles, the very people who put him in power. At a lavish banquet he assassinated them all. Then he went on to destroy the culture itself by eradicating the language. All government and business transactions from this day forward were to be done in Goidelic Gaelic only. As it was it took only ten years for the Pictish language to be removed from the system. Next he shut down Dunadd and moved his capital to central Pictland. Dal Riada and Pictland were now gone from this point on the land will be referred to as Alba. However, here is where he makes his one and only mistake. He does not put it writing. On paper Dal Riada and Pictland were still very much distinct countries. It isn't until years later (circa 930 AD) when we come across a Constantine II that Scotland is formally born.

With no fear of attack by the Vikings and a fully united country under one rule, Kenneth so typical of his time draws his attention to the Anglos. For the next 20 or some years he ravages Bernicia and Alt Clut. Kenneth is not interested in any political gains or territories; he has what he wanted now it's a simple case of pure unadulterated pillage. Bernicia is so economically ruined, for the Norseman to walk in is a piece of cake. Alba (formerly Dal Riada and Pictland) economically turns into a super power.

For Olaf of Dublin the union of the Scots and Picts gave him a much needed reprieve for he was for the longest time having enormous problems with the Danes. What he didn't need was attacks from Alba. However, by 870 AD Olaf was finally able to vanquish the Danes and with it he refocuses on Alba. Besides his young beautiful Scottish wife had become old and plain so he could care less of the marriage agreement. As it was he launched a major attack on the now Argyle territory only to be swiftly routed. Had he paid attention to the progress that Kenneth's exploits he would have realized Alba is a power not has been taken lightly. Alba now had an enormous well trained army that for 20 years could easily defeat any Anglo force. Taking on the Viking was not at all that difficult. For the first time the Vikings were no longer the undisputed masters of the region. They found themselves in much the same situation as all the former northern kingdoms were for the last 300 years. They would have to make allies if they were going make any progress from this day forward. As such they were in the same conundrum as all the other nations of the north; except for the time being Scotland.

Defeating the Vikings, Kenneth knew that was the big game changer. For the Vikings the tables had been turned around now they were the ones being hunted. And Kenneth was one of the first. For openers he wanted the Vikings out of Alba. The Vikings at this time had managed to penetrate into the mainland up in the north Fortriu region. In a very brief campaign Kenneth pushed them back onto the Orkney Islands. However, he was not interested in going any further. Burghead the harbor of the once enormous Pictish fleet had fallen to the Vikings a century earlier; so Kenneth he didn't have a navy to press his gains on the Orkney Islands.

Thus he decides to go in the other direction and push out the Vikings from the Shetlands. Again he has another easy victory over the Vikings. He has one last major engagement with the Vikings and of course that is at the great naval fortress of Burghead. It took the Vikings over two weeks to take the massive garrison so Kenneth knew up front this was not going to be easy and it wasn't. The chronicles don't say much on the fight only that Kenneth paid a high price for its recapture. Thus with Burghead once again returned to its rightful owners Kenneth decides to rebuild his navy.

Then according to the *Pictish Chronicles* Kenneth makes his first big mistake. With all his recent successes he decides to take his new fleet and pursue a series of attacks on Saxonia just west of Denmark. This venture turns into a disaster. The Danes retaliate and sack the Fortress Dunbar on the east coast just south of Burghead. Kenneth is forced to return home.

The blunder on the main continent had caused briefly a number of setbacks in Alba but of course Kenneth was quick to correct them all. Norseman again crossed into Alba from the Orkneys and the Shetlands but both were repulsed. Then the Picts who were dissatisfied with his reforms decide this is a good time to rebel. Tragically the revolt is quickly squashed. From all this we learn a little bit of Kenneth's personality. He has much the same characteristic as did Aengus of Munster did. He was ruthless when it came to any form of opposition. People learned very early in the game not to cross him. You have smile though that when you read the legends about him they paint a very different picture of him being a magnificent wonderful leader when in fact he was anything but.

Finally in 855 AD he was able to execute his biggest goal and that was to attack the Angles in Bernicia. Attack is what it was all about. Over the next five years he went on a campaign of looting. He was not interested in conquering only rape of the land and of all its wealth. However, his campaign like in Saxonia got off to a poor start. In the first two years the Angles easily repelled all his advances and things were getting demoralizing for his army again. Also, more rebellions broke out with the Picts so he had to temporarily call things off to again squash the rebellions. But then something happened. When he returned to Bernicia this time things were a lot different. He swept through the country side with complete ease raking in all sorts of booty to take home. Unfortunately when Kenneth returned from his last raiding adventure he fell ill and quickly died from a cancerous tumor. Not a very spectacular ending, he did leave Alba, later to become Scotland intact. On his death bed Scotland was now a solid nation all the way down to the Forth River. A few decades later it would be expanded all the way to Hadrian's Wall. And thus ended Pictland in the process.

Under normal circumstances the story should end here because Pictland is basically finished. But the truth is it isn't. Another major event occurs and that is when the fate of the Picts is sealed.

The year is 889 AD and a King Giric MacDungail is now the ruler of Alba (Scotland). He is the first ruler to come to the throne be way of linage and not selection. As it is we see firsthand the problems that comes with type of system. Giric was not at all a very competent leader.

The Vikings had come back and this time they were tearing up the land. Typically the Scottish nobles were growing in frustration for the lack of any effective leadership from the king. Since usurping the crown was no longer a serious offence we find Giric is assassinated by Aed Mac Cinaeda and of course he takes the throne by force. No surprise the Kingdom is put into an uproar and we have two boys Donald and Constantine II fleeing to Ireland. Some sources say Constantine was the son of Aed but there is lot of confusion on this point for others say he was the son of Giric. Donald was a cousin. Whatever is the true story the fact is both boys had to flee the country for their own safety. For ten years the boys were raised in Ireland as Aed ruled Scotland. Aed's leadership is described as one of corruption and his dealing with the Vikings was no more effective than that of Giric. In 899 AD the two boys returned to Scotland and in a brutal battle at Dumbarton, Aed was terminated. For a brief while Scotland was jointly ruled when Donald died in battle and Constantine II becomes the sole ruler.

Circa 900 AD a rather innocent event changes the history of Scotland completely, Constantine II wants things in Scotland to get some sense of semblance in the country again and with the national bishops, organizes a formal ceremony from which he becomes the legitimate ruler of Alba (Scotland). At a place called Scone that becomes forever recognized as the inauguration centre of kings Bishop Cellach prepares a document of oath for the first new king of a united country. The document is called, *"Paritier Cum Scottis"* meaning *"In Conformity with the Customs of the Gaels"*. This document formally and legally unites the two cultural halves of the country into one. Dal Riada and Pictland are once and for all dissolved and Scotland is born. From this date forward everything that pertains to the governing of the country is now addressed as Scotland.

And no sooner is Scotland born when the foundation is immediately threatened in probably the biggest battle to ever take place in the whole of Briton.

Meanwhile in Scotland there was still a series of conflicts under Kenneth MacAlpine and the rest of Briton was in a desperate fight with the Vikings. Northumbria and Cumbria were now completely consumed by the Norsemen and it was recognized by Alfred the Great as Danelaw. Alfred had started a campaign to slowly regain the lands taken by the Vikings but died before he could complete his mission. His sister Aethalflaed took over from him and successfully defeated the Vikings for the first time to have a completely united "England". When she passed away Alfred's grandson Aethalstan came to the throne. He was a dynamic Anglo king and he set out to unite all of Briton, north and south under one rule. He was very prolific when it came to writing treaties and contracts of commitment. Failing that he did not hesitate to march his army into countries like Wales and Cornwall to secure alliances. Finally in 926 AD he approaches both Scotland and the new kingdom of Strathclyde (formally Goddodin) to join his new kingdom of England. When Strathclyde succumbs to Aethalstan's pressure without a fight, Constantine basically alone also quickly signs an alliance with England. So no sooner is Scotland born when in a flash it is province of England. Almost seems tragic Scotland should disappear on the eve of its birth. However, everything is not what is seems. Once Aethalstan, who had brought an army up into Scotland and leaves Constantine renounces the agreement and declares Scotland's independence again.

Constantine had only 8 years (918 AD) earlier defeated a large Viking Army under King Ragnall of Danelaw and from it he knew the politics of the Norsemen were in the process of changing. Sure enough another King Olaf of Dublin came to power and immediately declared Danelaw now part of the Irish Viking Kingdom. With that King Owen of Strathclyde followed suit in 934 AD reverses his agreement with Aethalstan as well. The English ruler was completely caught off guard and couldn't collect an army of southern allies until a good three years later. In that time the three northern kings solidified their alliance and in a combine effort, march an enormous army of over 50,000 men into what was formally known as Bernicia. Aethalstan, though it is not recorded, the actual size of his army it is simply his forces were larger still. It is interesting the Battle of Hastings is the most renowned battle in the history of Britain and yet not more than 17,000 fought in it.

Two massive armies were slowly marching towards each other in 937 AD. The northern forces were heading in a south westerly direction towards Wales. There is a peninsula just north of Chester where the army swings north and stops about half way in an open field known as Brunanburh. Here they waited for the Anglo Saxon alliance to arrive. Finally Aethalstan arrives but he hasn't got all his forces together so he needs to stall. He meets with King Olaf and pretends that he is out manned by the northern armies and wishes to negotiate some form of treaty. After three days of senseless talks Olaf loses his patience and sends his army to ransack the country side. By this time Aethalstan's remaining armies arrive and he is posed for a fight.

On the first day of fighting Aethalstan marches in an organized broad front in what is called a locked shield formation. This style of formation was first used by Alfred the Great and proved to be very effective against the Vikings. The fighting goes on all day as men hack away at each other. The blood flowed like a river it was that terrible. Aethalstan could not budge the Vikings on his left flank but was slowly pushing the Scots and Strathclyde forces back. Yet as night falls there was no definitive win for anyone. Both armies somehow manage to break it off and return to their respective camps for the night.

The next day Aethalstan was the first to form up his armies on the open flat field. He reorganized his line to have his most experienced fighters in the front rank and he had his army in huge arrow shape formation. The idea he was going to pierce a hole into the enemy lines. The Northern army paid no attention to Aethalstan's strategy and once more formed up in a single long line and waited for the Anglo Saxon's to approach. When they clashed it was repeat of the day before. All day long the two armies hack away at each other with almost no effect on the outcome. One of the leaders of the Anglo Saxon forces fell in the afternoon and briefly Aethalstan's forces were collapsing all around him. Somehow he got a grip on things and the Anglo Saxons held. As the sun began to set likely out of sheer exhaustion the Scots and Strathclyde flank began to crumble and with it so too did the Vikings. Aethalstan keeping a firm grip did not exploit the opportunity he slowly marched forward and lost a brilliant opportunity. Soon the northern alliance was in a shamble and were literary running off the field. The Scots and the Strathclyde escaped over a nearby river and the Vikings who had their ships anchored at the tip of the peninsula quickly boarded them and set sail back to Ireland. Though Aethalstan clearly won the day there was not much left to his army. The Chronicles of the three leading countries all report casualties in excess of 80%. If we are to assume Aethalstan's army was around 60,000 when it started he ended with around 11,000 when the day was over. Plus you have to remember this is an army comprised of Welsh, Anglos, Cornish and Saxons. Marching home and going to their respective countries you have only a couple of thousands left. So it comes as no surprise that when Aethalstan got home himself he basically had nothing left to capitalize on his victory. As it was the united

England fell apart and for what this whole story is about Scotland survives.

CONCLUSION

As days turned into weeks, and weeks turned into months and months turned into years Constantine II waited patiently for the enviable end. Sounds like something out of a J.R.R. Tolkien story but in this case it was true. Constantine II was certain that it was only a question of time whether the Anglo Saxons would be back to finish the job or for sure face the assassin's knife. As we can well figure that after Kenneth Mac Alpine the times had changed. But neither event happened. Constantine II went on to live out his life and watched as his country once again evolved. All the former traditions of the Pictish Scots were now gone. Scotland now held its place with just about every other medieval kingdom throughout the whole of Europe. It wouldn't be long now when the country would be adopting yet another new trait and that being building enormous castles like the fame Edinburgh Castle. Even the language was to evolve with another, addition to it as well and that would be Latin brought on by the Roman Catholic Church. In 675 AD the fame Synod of Whitby would formally end the Celtic Christian Church and the fame monastic signature of the institution would quickly disappear. Some three year later when Edward I finally rolls into Scotland it's a changed land one that can easily fit in now with a Norman England. And I think that is probably the very best place to stop.

This book started with the statement that there is no mystery to the Picts and I think now that point is well established. The Picts emerged from the blend of two cultures that coexisted for some 400 years, in much the same way as the Anglos and the Saxons did in Briton. I think how it became was, most authors that I read start their stories of the Picts with when the Romans first arrive. As such by doing this we miss out on some 2000 years of evolution. The Urnfield People who are an essential part of the story are cut out of the picture and thus the existence of the Picts can't be explained properly. We have these strange tattooed people running around the country half naked and have this incredible ability to mystify the greatest war machine of the Roman Empire. Some 600 years later they are again doing it to the Anglos and the Irish Scots. Without knowing the two halves of the puzzle of course the Picts are fantastic mystery. The truth is, the Picts as we now know is taking that one step further into time, just as quick as we are to say they are a mysterious when we can equally say they are not.

Where the Picts became ingenious is obviously from their Urnfield People side. We know from Stonehenge the Urnfield People were a sophisticated race. When the Halstatt Celts arrived rather than subdue the people as was their typical custom across most of Europe they decide the embrace them. What evolves is a unique culture that is innovative and ferocious at the same time. By the time the Romans had reached the Firth of Forth they had figured the

Picts to be just another strange version of the Celts. What an embarrassing surprise it turned out to be. Emperor Severus who made the most determined effort to squash the Picts, exposes the extent of how culturally advanced the people had evolved into. They are well disciplined, organized people with and an enormous resilience to suffering. As such as we find in the "300 Year War" and later the Vikings, it is their staying power to survive. Scotland as we know goes on for yet another 1500 years when at last the British through the modern muskets at last conquer the nation. However, far too much time has passed and the Scottish culture of tartans and bagpipes is simply too deeply embedded to be so easily erased. The Scottish tradition is twice as old as the English and with far more determination in it.

BIBLIOGRAPHY

Anderson, A. O., *Adomnán's Life of Columba*, Oxford Press, Oxford, 1991

Aitchison, Nick., *The Picts at War*, Sutton Publishing, Stroud, 2003

Alcock, L., *The Neighbours of the Picts: Angles and Scots*, Roisemarkie, London 1993

Bain, Ian, *Celtic Knotwork*, Constable Publishing, London 1986

Barnes, Dr. Ian, *The Historical Atlas of the Celtic World*, Chartwell Books, Inc. New York, 2010

Bede, -The Venerable-, *The Ecclesiastical History of the English People*, Script, Northumbria, 673 AD

Bhreathnach, Edel , *The Kingship and Landscape of Tara*, Four Courts Press, Dublin 2005

Blond, Anthony, *The Private Lives of the Roman Emperors*, Running Press, London 2008

Clayton N. Donoghue

Breatnach, R.A. (translator), *The Book of Uí Mhaine*, lecture, Dublin, 1943

Byrne, E,J., *Niall of the Nine Hostages, (In Irish Kings and Queens)*, Oxford, London, 1973

Buel, Aubrey, *Megalithic Brittany*, Thomas and Hudson, London 1985

Cahill, Thomas, *How the Irish Saved Civilization*, Anchor Books, New York, 1995

Carver, Martin., *Surviving in Symbols; a visit to the Pictish Nation*, Osprey, Edinburgh, 1999

Chadwick, Nora, *The Celts*, The Folio Society, London, 2002

The Druids, University of Wales , Wales, 1997

Clark, Graham, *Prehistoric England*, F. E. Bording, London 1940

Clarkson, Tim, *The Makers of Scotland*, Birlinn, Edinburgh, 1988

Cumming, W.A., *The Age of the Picts*, Suttan Alan, London, 1995

Cunliffe, Barry, *The Celts, A very short Introduction*, Oxford University Press, London, 2003

Britain Begins, Oxford University Press, London, 2012

Curley, Walter, *Vanishing Kingdoms: The Irish Chiefs and their Families*. Lilliput Press. Dublin, 2004.

Delaney, Frank, *The Celts*, Grafton Books, London, 1986

Dewar, Michael, editor and translator. *Claudian - Panegyricus de Sexto Consulatu Honorii Augusti*, Oxford Clarendon Press, 1996.

180

Donoghue, C. N., *History of the Celts*, FriesenPress, Vancouver, 2013

The Irish Empire, FriesenPress, Vancouver, 2015

Dudley, Donald, *The Civilization of Rome*, Meridan Classic, Winnipeg, 1962

Dixon, Jack, *The Pict*, Standing Stone Press, New York, 2007

Eleure, Christine, *The Celts; The First Masters of Europe*, Abraham, New York, 1993

Ellis, Peter Berresford, *The Druids*, Eerdmans Publishing, Michigan, 1994

Fields, Nic, *Rome's Saxon Shore, AD 250-500*, Osprey Publishing, Oxford U.K., 2006

Foster, Roy (ed.), *The Oxford Illustrated History of Ireland*. Oxford University Press. 2001

Foster, Sally, *Picts, Gaels and Scots*, B. T. Batsford, England, 2012

Goldsworth, Adrian, *The Fall of the West: The Death of the Roman Superpower*, Weilfield & Nicolson, London, 2009

Grant, Michael, *The Fall of the Roman Empire*, Collier Books, New York, 1976

Gildas the Wise, *De Excidio et Conquestu Britanniae*, Script, Northumbria, 570 AD

Jackson, K.H., *The Evolution of the Goedelic Language*, British Academy, 1997

James, Simon, *The World of the Celts*, Thames and Hudson, London, 1993

Jonasson, Bjorn, *The Vikings*, Cudrum Publishing, London, 2008

Keating, Geoffrey with David Comyn and Patrick S. Dinneen (trans.), *The History of Ireland* (g) 4 Vols. David Nutt for the Irish Texts Society. London 1902–14Kinsella, T., (trans), *The Tain*, Oxford University Press, Oxford, 1969Konstan, Angus, *British Forts in the Age of Arthur*, Osprey Books, London, 2008

The Strong Holds of the Picts, Oxford, London, 2011

Konstan, Angus, *Strongholds of the Picts*, Osprey, London, 2010

Laing, Lloyd and Jenny, *The Picts and the Scots*, Sutton Publishing Ltd, Gloucestershire Stroud, 1994

Lavin, P., *The Celtic World*, Hippocrene Books Inc., New York, 1999

Livy, *The Early History of Rome*, trans. Aubrey de Selincourt, Penguin Books, London 1960

Mallory, J. P., *The Origins of the Irish*, Thames and Hudson, New York, 2013

Marcellinus, Ammianus, *Res Gestae*, trans, Kimberly Kagan, Yale, Connecticut 1972

Mathew, Caitlin, *The Celtic Tradition*, Elemental Book Limited, Rockport, 1995

MacAuley, Donald, (ed) *The Celtic languages*, Cambridge University Press, Cambridge, 2008

MacKillop, James, *Dictionary of Celtic Mythology*, Oxford University Press, New York, 1998

Mac Niocaill, Gearóid, *Ireland before the Vikings*. Dublin: Gill and Macmillan. 1972

Meyer, Kuno, *The Death of Niall of the Nine Hostages*, Oxford University Press, New York, 1900.

Molloy, J.P., *The Origins of Ireland* ,Thames and Hudson, London, 2010

Mountford, Paul Rhys, *Ogham*, Destiny Books, Vermont, 2001

Ó Cléirigh, Fr. Michael, *The Annals of the Four Masters*, Sligo, Ireland, 1632

O'Railly, T. F., *Niall of the Nine Hostasges*, Trinity Press, Dublin, 1946

Piggett, S., *The Druids*, Thames and Hudson, London 1968

Plutarch, *Makers of Rome*, trans. Ian Scott-Kilvert, Penguin Books, Harmondsworth, UK, 1965

Fall of the roman Republic, trans. Rex Warner, Harmondsworth, UK, 1958

The Rise of the Roman Empire, trans. Ian Scott-kilvert, Penguin Books, Harmondsworth, UK, 1979

Radston, Ian., *Celtic Fortification*, The Tempus Publishing Ltd, Gloucestershire, 2006

Rankin, H. D., *Celts and the Classical World*, Croom Helm, London, 1987

Richie, Anna., *The Picts*, Osprey, Edinburgh, 1989

The Kingdom of the Picts, Osprey, Edinburgh, 1995

Ridgeway, William., *"Niell of the Nine Hostages"* Junior Roman Studies, New York, 1924

Rodgers, Nigel., *The Roman World: People and Places*, Lorenz Books, London 2005

Salway, Peter., *The Oxford Illustrated History of Roman Britain*, Oxford, New York, 1993

Sutherland, Elizabeth., *In Search of the Picts*, Constable, London 1993

The Book of Ulster, 5th century - Author unknown, monastic

Venning, Timothy., *The Kings and Queens of Wales*, Amberley, Gloucestershire, 2012

Wagner, Paul., *Pictish Warrior*, Osprey, Oxford, 2002

Ward-Perkins, Bryan., *The Fall of Rome*, University of Oxford, New York, 2005

Weekly, T.H. (translator), *Pictish Chronicles*, Edinborough, 971 AD

Acknowledgement of Pictures

Pictures/Image Credits

Celtic Knots – blendspace.tres.com/lessen
Stone balls – Ashmodel Museum. U.K.
Brochs (2) – Internet Archaed. 19 Geddes
Pictish Stones (2) – Wikipedia, free encyclopedia
Burghead Fort – scothistoryonline.co.uk.
Hill Fort Wall – Wikipedia, free encyclopedia
Pictish Ship – pinterest.com
Orgham stone – prehistoricwaterford.com
Book of Kells – Theguardian.com
Brunanburh – Anglosaxontruth.weebly.com

CPSIA information can be obtained
at www.ICGtesting.com
Printed in the USA
BVHW042333280920
589810BV00008B/42

9 781460 292891